PUDDINGS TO PODIUMS

FROM FAST FOOD FAT MAN
TO ULTRAMARATHON CHAMPION

PUDDINGS TO PODIUMS

FROM FAST FOOD FAT MAN
TO ULTRAMARATHON CHAMPION

Nathan Flear

www.nathanflear.co.uk

Published in the United Kingdom.

Puddings To Podiums – From Fast Food Fat Man To Ultramarathon Champion

First Paperback Edition

ISBN: 9798865635888

To Tori, Skye, Summer, & Jackson.

Thank you for sharing this journey with me
and supporting me in chasing my goals x

Table of Contents

"Every morning in Africa, a gazelle wakes up. It knows it must run faster than the fastest lion or it will be killed. Every morning a lion wakes up. It knows it must outrun the slowest gazelle or it will starve to death. It doesn't matter whether you're a lion or gazelle. When the sun comes up, you'd better be running."

African Proverb

Prologue

"TEN MORE MILES, TEN MORE MILES," I REPEATED MY mantra as I pushed closer to safety. I was being chased down by the Gestapo, the relentless runner tailing me, desperate to catch me. Most had given up the chase hours ago, but this one runner just wouldn't let go, steadily closing the gap. I covered my headlamp, scanning the surroundings, hoping he wouldn't spot me so close. Every glance over my shoulder carried the expectation of his towering figure closing in. I looked again, shielding my light, searching for any sign of him doing the same, trying to sneak up and disrupt my game. I turned back and pressed on, my heart pounding, footsteps echoing in my ears. Was it him? I covered my torch once more, glancing back – only trees met my eyes. Don't stop, keep moving, I told myself. Ten more miles, ten more miles...

"He's two minutes behind!" a voice, of an angel, informed me at the last checkpoint. That was the moment I summoned my hidden reserves, a burst of speed that would later reduce me to a walk, but it had the same effect on him. The pain in my lead-filled legs became unbearable, but I had to block it out. There was no way I could stop now; he would catch me. I repeated the mantra to myself over and over, striving to drown out the pain.

Could he hear my footsteps? Could I hear his? Should I pause to listen or keep moving? I slowed to a walk, urging myself to go faster, but the pain made it difficult. How much distance was left? Panting heavily, glancing back and making sure to cover my headlamp, I wondered if he could hear my breath in the dark of the still night. My heart thumped vigorously inside my chest.

I asked the angel not to update me on his proximity anymore, and she respected my wish, only guiding me to water when my thirst became too much and offering words of encouragement when my spirit wavered. I knew she'd wait for me to reach the safe zone, and that thought fuelled my relentless rhythm, propelling me forward with every ounce of strength I had left.

At least the rain had ceased long ago. I couldn't have chosen a worse time to run – or so I had initially thought. The dampness of my shirt threatened to chill me to the core, rubbing against my skin like sandpaper over the miles. Thankfully, the sky had closed up again, creating near-perfect conditions. The night was cool, yet not painfully cold, and my constant movement kept me warm. I couldn't run fast or maintain a consistent pace anymore, but with so many miles behind us, I wouldn't need to. The Gestapo Officer must have been as fatigued as I was, so if I could maintain a steady stride, he wouldn't close the gap too quickly (or so I hoped).

I had embarked on this journey without much of a plan, relying on sheer determination to see me through. So far, it seemed to have worked, but the last ten miles were a gruelling slog, requiring me to dig deeper than ever before. Perhaps it was the knowledge that the end was drawing near. Yet, this wasn't the time for complacency. The Gestapo had trained just as hard as I had for this moment, and it would ultimately come down to who was most resolute. If my determination wavered for even a minute, I knew it would be a slippery slope – a slope I might not be able to ascend again. I pondered the consequences of letting him catch me, taking several deep breaths, steeling myself to once again run with unwavering strength.

Chapter 1

The Imagined Pursuit

FORTUNATELY, THE DANGER I PAINTED EARLIER WAS nothing more than a product of my exhausted mind during the Robin Hood 100 Miler. There was no actual Gestapo officer chasing me. The runner hot on my heels was none other than my friend Alistair Higgins, who happened to be my closest competitor in the race and has no nazi affiliation whatsoever. Oh, the wonders of a tired runner's imagination and the little mind games we sometimes play to keep us engaged and moving forward during these ridiculously long pursuits.

Now, the angelic presence that kept appearing by my side during that race was none other than my wife, Tori. She selflessly took on the role of my support crew, providing me with encouragement, nourishment, and that invaluable sense of love and belief.

I hadn't been a runner my whole life. Like many teenagers, I had my fair share of lofty goals. I daydreamed about becoming a pop star, envisioning myself harmonising with the likes of Take That.

Unfortunately, my vocal prowess was comparable to the cacophony of drowning cats. Later on, Football, had its grip on my imagination. I yearned to don the red shirt of Manchester United, but my skills fell short, as my brutally honest five-year-old son Jackson gladly attests.

Yet, one ambition shone brighter than the rest – the desire to join the army and become a war hero. The adrenaline rush of envisioning heroic feats pulsed through my veins. The rigorous fitness training for the parachute regiment felt natural. I seemed to breeze through challenges, fuelled by my regular five-mile runs and an unyielding determination. Even during the infamous bleep test, as others gasped for breath, I somehow held on, refusing to surrender. I believed that I was made for this, a long and distinguished army career was how I saw my future.

Fast forward to January 2nd, 2015.

Running was an unfamiliar territory to me. The past fifteen years had seen me neglecting this primal form of movement. But on that fateful day, Tori and I decided to take a jog together. We lived in a small Welsh village in Carmarthenshire, not too far from where I grew up, having recently returned from living in Malta, we had decided that we wanted our daughters Skye and Summer who were 5 and 3 at the time, to go to school in the UK, we were also struggling financially at that time, trying to make money online whilst working from home. We agreed that putting the children in School in the UK would give us the time and energy we needed to try and build a business and earn some money again.

That first mile on that cold January morning felt like a monumental struggle. Anyone passing by would have easily dismissed me as a typical January runner, coerced into the activity by his determined spouse. They might have wagered that I would swiftly retreat to the comforts of the sofa, my running gear forgotten and buried within the laundry basket until the next New Year's resolution. Our one-mile jog was a literal downhill battle, leaving us both gasping for air, doubled over, coughing uncontrollably. The daily five-milers of my past seemed like a distant memory, as if I had never run a step in my life.

It had only been a few months since I quit smoking – a habit that had engulfed me since my eighteenth birthday, chaining me to nearly forty cigarettes a day. Although I managed to kick the habit, I had replaced it with a vapor cigarette, puffing on it incessantly. It resembled a traditional cigarette and allowed me to puff away with a sense of familiarity. One coughing fit would barely end before I sought solace in the vapor once more. And let's not forget my attire – an ensemble consisting of baggy jogging bottoms, an oversized Manchester United hoodie, and ordinary training shoes – perfectly embodying the reluctant runner within me.

The innocent remarks of my friends about my weight had struck a chord deep within me. Years of neglecting exercise and indulging in food had led me to pile on the pounds, reaching just under 17 stone. While Tori was always kind and reassuring, I couldn't ignore the nagging feeling that something had to change. I wasn't quite sure how it had happened. We would bump into friends we hadn't seen for a long time and they'd say things like

"Wow, mate; she's feeding you well!"

I laughed it off but then later I could not get it out of my mind.

"Tori, have I really put on that much weight?" I asked.

"I can't see it myself," she replied, "I think they were exaggerating." She'd laugh and joke and say "They're probably talking about your massive muscles!" we'd laugh because I really didn't have massive muscles... or any muscles in fact.

Maybe she was just being kind. When I look back at photos now I can see that we'd both put on weight; me a lot more than her. When we saw each other every day at the time we didn't notice as much, but at the beginning of January 2015 I decided that enough was enough and I was going to get healthy. I was a father now, but I felt like I was setting a poor example by not looking after my health. Something had to change.

With a newfound determination, I embarked on a mission to get healthy. Tori and I decided to start our new regime by running a mile downhill. Of course, by running downhill we had shot ourselves in the foot a little bit, because the way back would all be uphill. Some might have been tempted to call a taxi, but at least we were willing to walk back up even if it was at snail's pace! We joked that people actually do this sort of stuff for fun! That incline felt like a mountain at the time. Nonetheless, we persevered. At 33, I couldn't blame my condition on the natural aging process. I hoped that with persistence, it would get easier, as I faintly recalled the feeling of fitness from my younger days.

The next day, I returned to the same route, establishing a daily routine that lasted for several weeks. Some days, I had to rest due to leg pain, similar to the aftermath of an intense first gym session after two decades of inactivity. Tori didn't join me every time, but she would accompany me every few days. Initially, I felt just as terrible at the end of each run, but gradually, something shifted. It became slightly easier. Encouraged by my progress, after a few weeks, I took on a three-mile "long run" around the local business park. Tori joined me, and together we completed it, maintaining a steady and unhurried pace. The scenery may not have been inspiring – just pavements and warehouses – but that was inconsequential. Our focus was on shedding weight and gaining fitness, and that's exactly what we were accomplishing.

Before long, I found myself regularly completing three to four-mile long runs, and my passion for running grew, I had well and truly caught the running bug. It consumed my spare time, as I delved into research, devoured running magazines, and eagerly discussed the subject with anyone who would listen. Tori, however, didn't share the same level of obsession. Shortly after we began our running journey, she became pregnant with our third child, which put her running on hold. Yet, my ambitions were soaring higher than just weight loss. I became a man on a mission.

Running brought me immense joy, and the weight started to melt away within a few months. If I'm honest I think Tori got a little bit sick of my new obsession, she was gaining weight with the pregnancy and I was losing more and more.

Early on, I stumbled upon an article about ultramarathons that ignited a fire within me. Among the races mentioned, one stood out like a beacon: The Spartathlon. This 153-mile race from Athens to Sparta in Greece captured my imagination like no other. Held annually in September, it had strict qualifying standards, making it a challenging endeavour for even the most accomplished ultra runners. But could I train hard enough to earn a spot on the British team for the Spartathlon? Could I represent Great Britain in any distance? I wondered if Wales had an ultra running team and what it would take to earn an international vest. Dreams and aspirations swirled in my mind as I became obsessed with pushing myself to achieve new heights.

Chapter 2:

The Goal

"TORI," I SAID EXCITEDLY, "THERE'S THIS INCREDIBLE race in Greece called 'Spartathlon.' It's a 153-mile race, and I've decided I'm going to run it!"

"mmm yes ok, that's great!" I don't think she was taking much notice of what I was telling her, she had probably switched off after hearing too much running talk,

"153 miles, I think I could run that with a bit of training, what do you think?"

Tori looked at me, "Did you just say 153 miles? Running?" she smiled and repeated "153 miles 1..5..3? how long do you get to do that... a month?"

I laughed and went to sit at the side of her to show her the article, "36 hours you get and a death bus follows behind picking up the ones who don't make the cut off" she could see I was getting excited just explaining it.

"That's horrific!" She said laughing, "It sounds like a horror movie! Death bus?"

We laughed and joked that she would have to crew for me, crewing would entail following the race in a car giving me drinks and food as and when needed, she'd say things like "can I drive with the death bus, it sounds more fun?" I don't think she ever thought I was serious about actually doing the race but I was! Running had become an all-consuming passion. I was determined to qualify for the Spartathlon.

Just a few months ago, running wasn't even on my radar. Now it consumed my every thought, and it did cause the occasional argument between Tori and me. She tried to be supportive, but running was more of a hobby for her, whereas it had become an obsession for me overnight.

Well I had a way to go before 153 miles was something I was actually capable of, but I thought I needed to set myself a goal to get things started. I stumbled upon an article in Runner's World magazine that rated races based on their goodie bags, and I couldn't help but drool over the descriptions. So, I decided to sign up for the Market Drayton 10k, which had been rated No1 for the best goodie bag.

As the race approached, my long runs had progressed to 6 miles. Completing a 10k didn't seem like a daunting task anymore. My goal for race day was to finish in under an hour, a target I was confident I could achieve. Tori and the kids, along with my mum and stepdad Stuart, came to cheer me on.

Standing at the start line, I felt a bit intimidated by the lean runners in club vests near the front. I sheepishly positioned myself at the back, among runners of my level. There were around 1,500 participants. The speakers blared Tina Turner's "Simply the Best," and the atmosphere was electric with spectators cheering along the course. The streets were lined with people, and random strangers praised my running form and I believed every word they said, it felt incredible,

From the beginning, I focused on maintaining a manageable pace, having read enough to know it was the best approach. I didn't want to get caught up in the adrenaline of the race and let my ego push me to try and overtake too many runners. I ran at a slightly quicker pace than my training, but it still felt comfortable. The entire experience was enjoyable. It was the first time I had been surrounded by so many other runners, and it gave me an indescribable buzz, a feeling that had been missing during my solitary training runs.

Just a few months ago, on January 2nd, running a downhill mile was a struggle. But here I was on May 10th, running over 6 miles without feeling completely drained. Could I really run Spartathlon? It was 147 miles longer, but people did it every year. The race had its roots in the story of a Greek messenger from ancient times called Pheidippides, and the first modern-day runners to attempt it were three British guys from the RAF. Inspired by the inspiring feat of Pheidippides, John Foden, John Scholten, and John McCarthy completed the route and created the race in 1983. Their determination and curiosity sparked the birth of the Spartathlon. In those early years, an unknown Greek athlete named Yiannis Kouros amazed everyone with his seemingly effortless performance, raising suspicions of cheating. But the following year, under intense scrutiny, Kouros proved his remarkable abilities and set a time of around 20 hours that remains unmatched to this day, Kouros went on to become a legend and the greatest ultra runner of all time.

Thoughts of the Spartathlon consumed my mind. However, I had to focus on the 10k race at hand before I could think about taking the next step toward Sparta. As I approached what I believed could be the final bend, I still felt strong and made a spontaneous decision. When I saw the digital finish clock, I couldn't believe my eyes. 48 minutes? It was far below my initial goal of finishing in under an hour. I summoned the last reserves of my energy and sprinted towards the finish line. Though exhausted, crossing that line filled me with overwhelming elation. Almost forgetting about the pork pie in my goodie bag, I revelled in the accomplishment. I was handed the bag by a friendly volunteer and as I turned around there stood Tori beaming with pride.

"That was brilliant! You did so well. I can't believe your time – 48:56 you did it in under 50 minutes!"

The realisation sank in, and I admitted to myself that it was a fantastic achievement for me. Eleven minutes below my target and finishing within the top half of the runners – it was beyond my expectations. Having started running only a few months ago, I wondered just how much faster I could become. But for now, I put those thoughts aside as the mouthwatering goodies in the bag beckoned me. In between bites, I answered my families questions, they all seemed proud of me, and Tori was especially full of praise. I think she was beginning to see that what I was doing might even inspire the kids to want to be healthy... the running, not the devouring of the pork pie that followed. She wanted to encourage me in my healthy new pursuit, although I don't think she realised at the time just how central to our lives it would become.

Later that evening, as I sat down for a brief moment, a sudden thought struck me. "I'll just stretch my legs a little so I don't stiffen up," I announced. Walking into the kitchen, I opened my laptop and delved into the world of online race calendars. It was time to seek out my next challenge.

I knew the road to Spartathlon would be long and demanding, but the taste of success in the Market Drayton 10k had only whetted my appetite for more. As I scrolled through race options, the possibilities seemed endless. Each race represented a new opportunity to challenge myself, to push beyond my limits, and to continue the incredible journey I had embarked upon.

With determination coursing through my veins, I selected my next race, knowing that it would bring me one step closer to the ultimate goal – Spartathlon. And as I closed my laptop, I couldn't help but feel a surge of excitement for the future that awaited me on those distant roads, leading me ever closer to the ancient city of Sparta.

Sitting there, I couldn't help but reminisce about the last time I became obsessed with an idea that would change my life. It was when I was 17, my planned military career cut short, and I was trying to figure out my next steps. Now, years later, that same fire burned within me. The burning desire to test my limits and discover what lay beyond them.

Chapter 3:

Let's Rewind

"THANK YOU, LINDA! I'M INCREDIBLY GRATEFUL," I replied, relieved that I wouldn't have to resort to flying back home that night. The weight of uncertainty lifted off my 17 year old shoulders as Linda handed me the keys to the room.

Settling into my temporary home, a small but cozy apartment, I took a moment to reflect on my journey so far. Qualifying for the army had boosted my confidence, but the subsequent medical discharge had left me feeling deflated. My knees, worn from the intense training at such a young age, had brought me to Tenerife in search of solace and a fresh start.

The flight had been nearly four hours long, and the early morning arrival time left me disoriented. Stepping outside the airport, I was greeted by darkness. Uncertain of what to do next, I decided to find comfort on a bench within the airport and let sleep take me.

Moments later, I was startled awake by a stern voice calling out, "Senor!... Senor!" Opening my eyes, I saw a beefy man in a green suit standing before me. A quick glance at his uniform revealed that he was from the Spanish Civil Guards.

"I'm going to Tenerife," I groaned, rubbing the sleep from my eyes.

"My friend, you are in Tenerife," he said tersely. "Please leave the airport!"

Realising my mistake, I couldn't argue with his request. The time on my watch indicated it was 8 am, so I must have managed a few hours of sleep. Stepping out into the Spanish morning, I immediately felt the scorching heat. The weight of my backpack added to my discomfort as I sought relief from the relentless furnace. Spotting a row of taxis nearby, I approached the first one.

"Playa de las Americas, Por Favor," I said with a smile, tossing my backpack into the cab.

"Ok, Ok," the taxi driver replied irritably. "Where do you want to go?"

Having stayed at the Orlando apartments in Torviscas before, I decided it would be a suitable place to start. The driver dropped me off, and I thanked him before paying the fare, eagerly anticipating a much-needed siesta.

However, my hopes were dashed when the lady at the reception informed me, "Sorry, sir. There is nothing available."

Undeterred, I remembered another nearby hotel and hoisted my backpack onto my back, trudging toward it. Unfortunately, the same response greeted me once again: "Sorry, sir. There is nothing."

This pattern persisted for several hours, gradually eroding my optimism. I began to entertain the idea of flying back home that very night if I couldn't find a place to stay. With around the equivalent of £160 pounds in Spanish Pesetas, it would be enough to cover the cost. Feeling parched from the heat and the arduous search, I stumbled upon a nearby bar and treated myself to a refreshing glass of cold beer. The cool liquid rejuvenated my spirits as I sat on the stool, savouring each sip.

Engaging in conversation with the friendly barmaid, who happened to be from the north of England, I shared my predicament. She sympathised, acknowledging the busy nature of the season. Then, a glimmer of hope emerged as she mentioned an English lady named Linda, residing in the apartment block across the road.

Eager not to let this opportunity slip away, I left a bit of my beer unfinished and hastily made my way to Linda's apartment. As I arrived, I quickly found her. Despite her being older than I had imagined, her friendly demeanour and warm Birmingham accent put me at ease.

"Linda, I hope you can help me," I began, exuding a mix of desperation and relief.

"I've been searching all over for a place to stay, but there's nothing available. Do you happen to have any rooms?"

A smile graced Linda's face as she replied, "I do, love. In fact, you're in luck. One of the rooms just became available."

I couldn't contain my gratitude as I let out a heartfelt, "Thank you!" However, my elation quickly waned as Linda mentioned the price.

"It's £200 for the week," she stated matter-of-factly, causing my grin to fade.

Trying to hide my disappointment, I murmured through clenched teeth, "Ah, right. The thing is, I've only got £150. You see, I planned to find work as soon as I arrived, but that's all I have at the moment. I don't know if..."

But before I could finish my sentence, Linda's warm smile reassured me. "Don't worry, love," she said kindly. "You can stay for the first week for £140. After that, it'll be the usual rate."

Relief washed over me once more, and I couldn't help but feel grateful for Linda's understanding and generosity. With a renewed sense of hope, I handed her the £140 and accepted the key to the room.

Entering the modest yet cozy apartment, I took a moment to appreciate the newfound stability. It may not have been the smoothest start to my time in Tenerife, but at least I had a place to call home for the next week.

As I settled into the room, my mind began to wander, contemplating the twists and turns that had led me here. My journey from the army to Tenerife had been marked by highs and lows, testing my resilience at every step. Yet, despite the setbacks, I found solace in the fact that I had embarked on a new adventure, a chance to redefine myself and discover what lay ahead.

Little did I know that this temporary refuge in Tenerife would become a pivotal chapter in my life. The experiences, friendships, and challenges that awaited me would shape the person I was to become and guide me towards a future I could have never envisioned.

But for now, as I closed my eyes and drifted into a much-needed sleep, I allowed myself to bask in the relief and gratitude of having found a place to rest my weary body. Tomorrow would bring new possibilities, and I was ready to embrace them with open arms.

The fact that I only had £10 left in my pocket hardly mattered. Thanks to Linda, I could stay here, and I was certain I would find some sort of work soon. The concern of paying next week's rent was a distant worry, something I would tackle when the time came. After a refreshing dip in the pool and a quick shower, I ventured out to explore the town and seek job opportunities. Tenerife boasted an abundance of bars, and I was convinced that at least one of them must be in need of a bartender. Yet, my initial bar-hunting experience mirrored my earlier search for accommodation; disappointment followed me as I went from one place to another, being told there were no openings. Just as hope was beginning to dwindle, I stumbled upon the Millennium pub. Stepping inside, I was abruptly transported from the scorching Spanish sun into a dimly lit English tavern.

My senses readjusted, and I was greeted by the voice of a middle-aged Londoner with the rosiest cheeks I had ever seen.

"What can I get ya, son?" he grumbled.

Trying my best not to be mesmerised by those cheeks, which bore the marks of a lifetime's heavy drinking, I replied,

"Well, I was actually hoping you might have some work available."

"Ah! You'll have to speak to my manager about that, and he'll be here around 8. Wanna come back then?" he offered.

"Ok, cool," I responded, my spirits lifted by the prospect of a potential job. Not lingering for a drink, I decided to head back to the apartment and use the remaining hours to prepare for a possible interview. Although I hadn't received an official offer yet, the bartender, whose name I later learned was Alan, had encouraged me to return. That alone gave me hope. I refrained from visiting other bars because The Millennium somehow felt like a place I'd fit in. However, hunger gnawed at my stomach, and with approximately £5 left in my pocket, I knew it was enough for a burger and a bag of crisps to sustain me. After satisfying my hunger, I lounged by the pool, enjoying another swim, until suddenly, it was half-past seven, and the time had come to make my way back to meet the manager. As soon as I walked into the pub, Alan recognised me from earlier.

"Ah, Nathan," he said, "I'd like you to meet Ali, the manager of this fine establishment!"

Grinning, Ali extended his hand and said, "Ah, good to meet you, Nathan. I've heard you're looking for work."

We engaged in a lively conversation for about 20 minutes, and Ali struck me as a decent guy. At 25 years old, he seemed incredibly mature to my 17-year-old self. Originally from Southampton, he had been living in Tenerife for five years and appeared to have found success. Suddenly, during a lull in our conversation, Ali poured four pints of vodka and Red Bull, each with a straw. He placed three in front of me and kept one for himself.

"Have a drink, Nathan," he offered, sipping his own through the straw. Throughout the entire time, his eyes never left mine, indicating that I should follow suit. As a teenager with hardly any money left,

I appreciated the free drink. However, back home, I couldn't legally order a pint, and now I was handed a pint-sized concoction of vodka and Red Bull. I eagerly indulged, swiftly finishing mine around the same time Ali finished his. Without pause, he placed another pint in front of me, and we repeated the process. Looking back now, I realise that this was my interview. I downed those two pints in record time and managed to remain upright and coherent. Ali took it as a sign that I would be suited for this place.

"Right, you can start now," he declared.

"Oh... fantastic!"

"You'll earn 2 million Pesetas a night (equivalent to around £8) and have all the free alcohol you can handle."

"Sounds good to me!"

I had no idea how my wages would cover Linda's rent, but I was confident I'd figure it out. For now, I had a roof over my head, a job, and free drinks and crisps to keep hunger at bay.

My role involved being a PR person for the bar, but it wasn't an office-based job. Essentially, I had to stand outside and entice people to come in. My training involved observing Ali and mimicking his techniques, which was truly eye-opening. Driven by my desire for money, I aimed to bring as much business to the bar as possible, impressing Ali and potentially unlocking new opportunities. His approach was mesmerising to witness. He persistently approached people passing by, not giving up until they agreed to come in for "just one drink." But he did it with such cheek and charm that they couldn't help but like him. After observing his magic a few times, I began employing the same tactics, bolstered by the pints of vodka and Red Bull that gave me the confidence to do so. It was astonishing how often it worked.

If someone managed to bypass us, they would be immediately accosted by touts from the next bar, ultimately forcing them to say yes to one of them. This job marked the beginning of a wild chapter in my life. At that time, my sole desire was to excel at everything I did. You could say that this drive has stayed with me throughout the years and has been one of the driving forces behind my overly ambitious dreams.

In the years that followed, this lifestyle continued, with an endless supply of alcohol and freedom. I made the decision to forgo returning to the army and instead live it up in Spain.

I embarked on a journey through various bars and eventually found my way to call centres, where I excelled as the top seller by applying Ali's charming and friendly tactics. I earned some money from this and was able to invest, leading to more lucrative opportunities. Along the way, I met like-minded friends through different jobs, which inspired me to start organising bar crawls and boat parties. I assembled a team of young and enthusiastic ticket sellers, reminiscent of my own early days. Each ticket sold for £25, with £15 going to me and £10 to the seller. We often sold around 300 tickets for a single event, doing this three nights a week. Through our endeavours, I went from struggling to pay my weekly rent to comfortably earning thousands of pounds a week – an unimaginable amount of money for me at the time.

Later on, I ventured into property sales and development, even owning racehorses, including Sarah's Art, the winner of the Grey's

Race at Newmarket, that was a special day at the races. I had an executive box at Old Trafford, hung out with celebrities, footballers, and gangsters, dined with Tito Jackson and his mother at their LA home shortly before his brother Michael's tragic passing, and even made headlines in the News of the World when an undercover reporter attended one of our boat parties. By the time I reached 23, I was making more money than I could fathom, and I felt like I was on top of the world. However, I couldn't have been more mistaken. I had unknowingly entered a murky and superficial world. The fit and healthy teenager who had once joined the army had transformed into a chain-smoking, hard-drinking substance abuser with more money than sense. I was hurtling towards self-destruction. My escalating cocaine habit, coupled with other destructive behaviours, threatened to consume me.

Everything changed one day when 'Crazy Gary,' a "security guy" who had insinuated himself into working for my business partner and me, showed a rare moment of loyalty by giving me a tip-off that saved my life.

"Nathan, you're in serious trouble," he warned. "The paddy gangsters overheard you at the bar last night boasting about your cash in the bank, and they want it. They asked me to help them get it, but I refused. However, if it's not me, someone else will step in. They plan to kidnap your girlfriend and hold her for ransom. If I were you, I'd disappear."

This revelation shattered my invincibility, abruptly bringing me back to reality. I had ventured far beyond my depth. Paranoia fuelled by drugs heightened my awareness, and I knew I had to leave immediately. Me and my girlfriend at the time, hastily packed a suitcase, and together we drove to the other side of the coast. We were living on the Costa del Sol, infamously known as the 'Costa del Crime,' and I had become dangerously complacent. My arrogance and shallow lifestyle were unsustainable. If I continued down this path, I would meet an untimely demise. It was time to bid farewell to Spain. There was no bravado, no thought of gathering Crazy Gary and others to confront the gangsters. I simply had to get away.

Of course, this is just a brief summary of a significant chapter in my life. I am far from proud of who I used to be, and I have only touched the surface to provide context for what followed. I was young, and like many, I made mistakes. However, these mistakes could have easily cost me my life and took a severe toll on my health. I don't know what would have happened if I had stayed in the army. Perhaps that path would have also led to my demise. Nevertheless, leaving the army set in motion a series of events that, while they may make for compelling anecdotes, are not the focus of this book.

The person I was in Spain is almost unrecognisable to me now. He was a product of youthful idealism, misguided ambitions, and negative influences. I lost the fortune I had amassed during that time, that's another story too, but Tori, assures me that she prefers the man I have become over the man I was back then. In the end, everything came full circle, and the values my mother instilled in me resurfaced after being overshadowed by greed and youthful arrogance.

The experience in Spain took a dramatic turn when I was forced to flee for my safety. At that time, I had no idea what running away would signify in my life. However, as I would do again later on in life, once I started running, I never looked back. It marked a pivotal moment of change and self-reflection. I realised that I needed to leave behind the destructive path I had been on and rediscover the person I truly wanted to be.

I hope that this part of my story serves as a cautionary tale, illustrating the consequences of unchecked ambition and misplaced priorities. My transformation from that reckless young man in Spain to the person I am today has been a profound journey of growth, humility, and redemption. It is my sincere hope that through this story, others can find inspiration, strength, and the resolve to make positive changes in their own lives.

Chapter 4

Into the Unknown

I WAS ON A MISSION TO SET MYSELF A NEW challenge, something to surpass the half-marathon I had recently signed up for. There was an itch to accomplish more, and that's when the idea of the Spartathlon took hold of my thoughts. The concept of training for years for such a race seemed daunting, but I had to make up for lost time – all those years of neglecting fitness, my body and my health. And so, I began sifting through races online, searching for the perfect challenge. It was then that the Chiltern Challenge 50k caught my eye. It wasn't just slightly longer than a marathon, it was longer than anything I had run before, including a half-marathon which was just a month away. But hey, if I could finish a half-marathon, then 50k didn't sound too far-fetched. So, the next thought was simple – better start training, and training hard.

My legs felt like they'd been through a marathon the morning after the Market Drayton10k race. It made sense to take a breather for a few days, to let those muscles recuperate. However, I was no advocate for sitting idly, and a few days felt like enough. My focus shifted towards stretching my long-run distance. The thought of running a half-marathon was a bit intimidating; heck, I wasn't even sure if I could run the entire distance. But I comforted myself with the idea that if push came to shove, walking wouldn't be the end of the world. It was a plausible plan. My studies kept their relentless pace, and a common theme seemed to emerge in the running world – a strategy for running a half-marathon. Most articles sang the same tune: go slow for the first 11 miles, then unleash everything you've got for the final 2, throw the kitchen sink at it. The mental image of lifting and hurling a kitchen sink after 11 miles stuck in my mind.

Standing at the start line, I repeated my "kitchen sink mantra." The idea was to go slow in the beginning, save up for the final burst. That seemed reasonable, considering I had something left in the tank at the 10-mile mark during my training runs. The race kicked off, and that mantra "throw the kitchen sink" echoed in my head. It gave the early miles a sense of purpose. I maintained what felt like a manageable pace, without a clue about my projected finishing time. I had an estimated goal of around 2 hours in my head, but this was uncharted territory. I was conscious not to let the time dominate my thoughts.

At the 10k mark, I found myself reflecting on how a month ago, it had been the finish line. Such shifts in perspective felt like a reflection of life's ever-changing challenges. But now, my sights were set on greater distances. My training had changed my perception of what was achievable. I was learning that hard work could convert lofty dreams into tangible realities. The race continued, and each passing mile was a testament to my progress. The 8-mile point, then the 9, came and went, and I was holding a steady pace. With just four miles remaining, I mentally readied myself for that final push – the kitchen sink moment.

As I neared that pivotal juncture, I found myself picturing not just the phrase but the actual kitchen sink. The sheer absurdity of it fuelled my determination. The finish line was drawing closer, and with each step, I envisioned hurling that metaphorical sink with all my might. The moment of reckoning was upon me. The last bend arrived, and there they were – Tori and the kids, a visual reminder of why I was pushing myself so hard. I poured everything into that final stretch, overtaking a couple of other runners. Crossing the finish line, I was taken aback – my time was 1 hour and 50 minutes.

Tori's words of praise filled the air. "You finished well under 2 hours!" she exclaimed with infectious enthusiasm. I was indeed proud of myself, but the ever-competitive spirit within whispered that I could have gone faster. The little ones might not have fully grasped the magnitude of my achievement, but their excitement was palpable.

As I sat in the car later, rummaging through the post-race goodies, a packet of salty crisps caught my eye. In that moment, those crisps tasted like victory itself. Yet, my mind swiftly shifted to the upcoming 50k race, just a month away. Anticipation mingled with determination; a heady cocktail that made me eagerly look forward to my next challenge.

But, before I could get to the 50k challenge, there was another race that demanded my attention – the Caerphilly 10k on Father's Day in 2015. It felt like a perfect way to celebrate. The plan was simple: go out there, soak in the experience, and enjoy every step. My speedwork in training had been a bit ad hoc, not structured, but I was naturally gaining pace as my weekly mileage increased.

Oddly, the 10k distance didn't seem as intimidating as it once had; I was evolving, and psychologically, it seemed time to toss that metaphorical kitchen sink into the mix a bit earlier. The race didn't carry any pressure, rather it felt like a festivity. My daughters crafted a poster for me that read, 'Go on daddy, happy Father's Day!', and as I hit the road, I was free from any time-related anxiety. The Caerphilly route was notably flat, and it offered plenty of delightful distractions: a monumental cheese sculpture, a Tommy Cooper statue, and, of course, the famous castle, an ever-present landmark during a good part of the route. Crossing the finish line, my thoughts were consistent – I could have gone faster. Nevertheless, I had improved my time to about 45 minutes, indicating progress. The question now lingered; how much faster could I get?

As my training regimen evolved, I temporarily parked my speed ambitions, shifting my focus to the upcoming 50k challenge. For this race, the key was pacing, not speed bursts. A 50k, or 31 miles, was nearly 20 miles more than I had ever covered in one run. It struck me that attempting a longer training run would be prudent. Coincidentally, we were headed to my mums in Herefordshire a few weekends before the race. An idea sprang to mind – I could run part of the journey, while Tori and the girls would drive and meet me later. The town of Llandovery, around 20 miles from home, was conveniently along the way and became my designated point to pause. To make this adventure possible, a backpack was essential. It needed to carry the supplies to sustain me during this epic run. A few packs of fruit pastilles and SPAR's own version of a Lucozade sport drink were my chosen rations. As for the backpack, practicality trumped brand names. Instead of splurging on a high-end, ultra-lightweight model, I settled for a £7 bargain from eBay, a choice that made perfect sense to me.

As I loaded up my supplies into the backpack, the sense of embarking on a journey, an adventure, excited me. The imagery of me meeting my family, after completing this ultra-run, felt almost like a rendezvous in an action movie. I imagined saying, "Meet me at the extraction point in four hours," with the "chopper" being a car parked at a pub. With enthusiasm fuelling my steps, I set off, unaware of the slight miscalculation in my backpack strategy. The contents started bouncing around like kids on a bouncy castle, first mildly amusing, then increasingly irritating. Despite this minor annoyance, there was no turning back now. And as I jogged on, I reminded myself, don't pick up the pace at 11 miles, just stick to the plan. Surprisingly, it was fairly easy to maintain a steady pace, and I found myself covering ground with greater ease than expected. Roughly three hours later, I arrived at the pub car park. I quickly calculated that if I could finish a marathon in about 4 hours, then completing a 50k in 5 or 6 hours was a reasonable goal. The 20-mile run felt good; 31 miles didn't seem too daunting at all.

"It's just another challenge," I told myself, "If I can't run, I'll walk. I'll get it done."

Having a bit of time before meeting my family, I ordered a small beer and claimed a table outside. That beer was nothing short of divine – a refreshing change from the now-warm sports drink I had been consuming for hours. As I savoured the moment, waiting for them to arrive, my thoughts dwelled not on what I had seen or felt during the run, but rather on the impending 50k. It couldn't come soon enough. Tori, as usual, was quick to laud my 20-mile run, assuring me that the 50k would be a piece of cake. But as mothers do, my own mum was more cautious.

"50 kilometres, Nath? Are you sure about this?" her eyes danced with concern.

"Yeah, mum, don't worry. I just ran 20 miles. 50k isn't that much farther."

"It just sounds like such an immense distance."

Her concern, while endearing, couldn't overshadow my determination. A few weeks ahead of the 50k, I purchased a tent and some camping equipment. I saw an opportunity to transform the experience into a mini-adventure. The night before the race, we settled into a campsite near Princess Risborough in the Chilterns, an idyllic setting nestled among hills and complemented by a charming country pub. It was a picture-perfect scene, matching all my expectations. Our dinner for the evening was a hearty lasagne from the pub – the new cooking gear remained unused, given the pub's convenient culinary offerings. I sipped a couple of beers to complement the meal, though my days of excessive pub visits had waned. Fatherhood left little time for such indulgence, and my priorities had changed. While I had drifted apart from old friends, I had rekindled my friendship with Rhys, an old schoolmate. He had kept himself in shape over the years, and our coffee chats evolved into discussions about training. Nights of raucous revelry were now part of a bygone era.

With a satisfying fullness and a calming ambiance, I lay down to rest that night. The company of my family was my true wealth now. On the morning of the race, excitement bubbled within me. I was immersed in the vibrant atmosphere, surrounded by an eclectic mix of fellow runners at the registration. Athletes ranged from looking like seasoned professionals to those who seemed less athletically inclined, echoing the spectrum of characters you'd find in any road race. My goal was not to race to the front; instead, I was assigned to the first wave, designated for slower runners. In hindsight, it seemed like anyone they estimated to finish over six hours were placed in this wave. I intended to start from the very back and simply see where the day took me. If the others raced ahead, that was fine; I would adhere to my pace, knowing it should carry me to the finish within the cutoff time, as long as disaster didn't strike. Like my first 10k race, I had a strong sense that I would finish, so my aim was to soak in every bit of the experience.

It was time to bid Tori and the girls a temporary farewell, though I knew they would be waiting for me at various points along the route, and the thought of those meetups added a pleasant anticipation to the race. I took my place at the back of the pack, and after a swift briefing, the race began. The early moments involved tackling quite a few steps, and forming a slow-moving procession. I couldn't find my running rhythm in this section, so I was content to walk the steps, allowing my legs to warm up gently. I planned to make up for lost time once the ground levelled out. The stairs might have felt like a ten-minute stroll, but I didn't mind.

During those initial miles, I maintained a leisurely pace, indulging in chats with fellow runners. In time, I would discover that ultra races carried a distinct social aspect not often found in shorter races. Perhaps, in the shorter races, everyone's pushing too hard to engage in conversation, but in ultras, it's a different story. Only the front-runners are truly pushing it, leaving ample room for chatter throughout the field. I didn't specifically mention how long I'd been running, but I did share that this was my first ultra – a sentiment echoed by several of us that day. While some might not consider 50k a full-blown ultra, arguing it's just a bit more than a marathon, for me, it most certainly counted.

One of the joys of ultras, a feature distinct from shorter races, was the aid stations. By then, I'd lost a considerable amount of weight, shedding down to around 12 stone or 76kg. It was evident in every photograph – a stark contrast from before. This change meant that my trips to the aid stations were a guilt-free indulgence. Tori and the girls appeared at each station, a motivating sight.

A fellow runner pointed out Chequers, the Prime Minister's retreat, as we wound our way around. The mansion was a picture of grandeur, quite unlike the tent that would host me later. Conversations with fellow runners transformed the stretches between aid stations into more enjoyable segments. Even during lulls in conversation, the stunning landscapes provided ample visual delight. My choice of race had proved wise – the Chilterns showcased the picturesque charm of the British countryside.

When the aid stations appeared, I made full use of them, taking a couple of minutes to savour the offered treats. My family's presence was a constant morale boost, though they had to contend with the considerable competition posed by the Haribo for my attention. I distinctly recall stuffing my pockets with them, relishing those sweet pick-me-ups throughout the run. These stations became islands of culinary joy amidst the endurance challenge.

As the race progressed, I could feel the miles wearing on me, and the unknown terrain past the 20-mile mark revealed itself. This wasn't a surprise; I'd read many accounts of ultra races, preparing me for these moments. I braced myself, ready to push through this phase. My feet had been throbbing for a while, and I suspected I had developed a few blisters. It was a new challenge for me in a race – fatigue creeping in before the finish line. I'd read about the emotional highs and lows that often mark the ultra experience. This was it – the uncharted low, the infamous 'wall' others had described. But I was prepared. I knew I had to grit my teeth and persist, one step at a time. This was exactly the challenge I had signed up for. So, head down, I trudged forward, each step an effort, every footfall a test of my willpower. The aid stations offered brief respites, and the Haribo, my trusty companions, accompanied me on this arduous journey.

As the finish line loomed ahead, I tried to summon a final burst of energy, though I suspect it was more of a shuffle than a sprint. My feet were now a symphony of agony, but the knowledge that a proper rest was just steps away propelled me forward. Tori and the girls were there, their cheers enveloping me like a victorious embrace. Crossing the finish line marked a shift within me. Unlike the 10k or the half-marathon, which I could envision conquering even at the start, this felt like an enormous triumph. I limped over to a spot away from the course and slowly lowered myself onto the grass. With my eyes briefly closed, a sense of achievement and relief washed over me. When I reopened them, my grin grew even wider, my spirits lifting as I spotted Tori extending a chilled can of Kronenbourg toward me.

"You did it, Nath!" she radiated, her pride tangible. "You're incredible! We're so proud of you."

As I cracked open the can and tasted the first sip, it was like a liquid embodiment of the crisp packet from my first half-marathon finish. The golden elixir seemed to course through my veins, alleviating the blisters on my feet and cooling me from the inside out. Oh, it was heavenly!

My finish time read 6 hours, 20 minutes, and 56 seconds, perhaps a bit slower than my initial musings in the pub car park after that gruelling training run. But now, with the firsthand knowledge of the multifaceted nature of ultras, I understood how countless variables could affect your pace, something not as prominent in shorter races. Despite that, I secured the 66th spot out of 193 finishers, comfortably in the top half. I remained seated on the grass for a while, relishing my Kronenbourg, exchanging thoughts with Tori and the girls about the race, and applauding fellow runners as they triumphantly crossed the line. The entire event exuded an inclusive and amicable atmosphere, solidifying my desire to be a part of this world.

Finally, we headed back to the campsite, where we basked in the evening sun. It was one of those days that seemed reluctant to end. Recollecting my past self in Spain, I realised that this life, this sense of fulfilment, was infinitely richer. Money, while important, held a different place now. If I had enough to get by, that was more than sufficient. Shedding around 5 stone since the journey began on January 2nd, transforming from someone who got out of breath running a mile into a 50k finisher in a mere six months, reinforced my belief that with dedication, almost any goal is within reach.

Morning arrived, and I stirred from my slumber on the unforgiving ground within my sleeping bag. Attempting to move proved more of a struggle than I'd anticipated. A novel soreness permeated my legs, a sensation beyond anything I'd felt before.

"I think it's going to be a while before I'm up," I grimaced, and Tori chuckled.

Eventually, I managed to extract myself from my makeshift bed.

By the time night rolled around again, my eyes were already scanning the horizon for the next undertaking. The feeling of triumph I had experienced after the 50k was addictive, akin to a drug. Perhaps this was my own form of an addictive personality. As long as I managed it responsibly, this newfound pursuit had to be positive.

Soon after, the Gower 50 Miler caught my attention. With ample time to recover from the 50k and then train for this new challenge, I was eager to delve into an even greater ordeal. 50 miles – an astonishing distance! While I genuinely couldn't predict whether I'd succeed, the accomplishment of the 50k provided a glimmer of hope that I might be up to the task.

My thirst for knowledge knew no bounds. I devoured a plethora of reading materials about running – training theory and strategies, dietary approaches, sport psychology, detailed race accounts, and practically anything that I could fit into my schedule. An intriguing realisation dawned on me: through all my research, I had essentially been coaching myself. Although my running journey was just six months young, an idea started taking shape in the recesses of my mind. While it was too early to take it too seriously, the concept began to germinate. With the substantial knowledge I was amassing, could I potentially become a running coach? Running, which had quickly overtaken my life, was beginning to provide me with more joy than anything else had thus far. It consumed my thoughts during every free moment, becoming a kind of newfound religion.

As my understanding of the Gower 50 Miler deepened, so did my understanding of the enormity of the challenge ahead. Unlike the Chiltern Challenge, this race seemed like a whole different league. Opting for a 50-mile debut might not have been the easiest choice. Comparing my anticipated completion time to the previous challenge, I estimated that the Gower 50 would likely demand at least 4 hours more of my endurance. This prompted a slew of new considerations: would I need more substantial fuel during the race? Could I anticipate numerous peaks and valleys in my energy levels, and how would I manage them? Was it even feasible to contemplate walking when I reached that daunting 40-mile mark? The magnitude of the upcoming challenge was certainly not lost on me, but far from deterring me, it only heightened my enthusiasm for the task at hand.

Chapter 5

A New Kind of Love

WITH TORI AND ME, THE PERSON I WAS BACK THEN meant that our initial meeting in Spain carried its share of obstacles. Looking back, I think fate played a hand in keeping us apart back then. Our first meeting had been while we were both involved in other relationships. At that time, I definitely fancied her, but our existing relationships set clear boundaries for any potential connection. Fast forward, and destiny seemed to offer another chance. After I'd returned to the UK, a friend of mine in Manchester mentioned he was meeting up with Tori. We'd all worked together in Spain, and he was kind enough to allow me to join. This unexpected reunion reignited my attraction to her, and things took off from there.

Right from the beginning, we just clicked. The beauty of those early days was that we felt comfortable around each other, even with the added catalyst of drinks and lively meals. Tori exuded a magnetic and infectious sense of fun, and I found myself wanting to spend more and more time with her. In those moments, distractions faded away, as I'd lost touch with many friends from Spain and social media wasn't the force it is today. This unique opportunity allowed Tori and me to truly get to know one another without the interference of outside influences.

Soon, matters took a serious turn, as Tori became pregnant with Skye, our firstborn. While it wasn't part of the plan, I was ready for the responsibilities of fatherhood. I'd always contemplated the kind of father I'd become, wanting to provide everything I'd wished for from my own dad. My lifestyle would need an overhaul; I had to cut back on the partying habits. Since I'd started my life in Spain, I'd maintained a steady rhythm of revelry. However, Tori's pregnancy was like a gentle yet firm reminder that it was time to leave the party and embrace the responsibilities of fatherhood. If there was a devil whispering in my ear, it wasn't strong enough to compete with the resolute call for change.

But, don't be fooled, my transformation was instantaneous. Like the state I found myself in after that first run, the changes didn't occur overnight. I still occasionally enjoyed a night out and struggled with impulsive food consumption – a weakness that persists to this day, although it's under much better control. Presently, I reward myself with treats after particularly demanding runs or significant races, but for the most part I maintain a sensible diet.

Most importantly, my priority became about my little family, ensuring I'd always be there for them. This commitment deepened with the arrival of Summer, our second daughter, and intensified further when Jackson, our son, joined our family. My family is my anchor, the true axis around which my world revolves. In the present day, we've opted for homeschooling, and I've managed to arrange a work-from-home setup. This grants me the luxury of spending most of my time with my family, just enough hours to get my work done, and the remaining four or so hours per day dedicated to running.

Some might find this amount of time with their kids overwhelming, but I'm at the opposite end of the spectrum. If I ever have to leave for a race or other commitment, a sense of apprehension inevitably creeps in. I recognise that this attachment might not be entirely healthy. I'm occasionally concerned that we might be too close, considering the quantity of time we spend together. Moreover, part of my motivation comes from a determination to create a different kind of father-child relationship than the one I experienced growing up.

My dad left me and my mum when I was just 2 years old and had very little influence on my childhood. I was determined this wouldn't be the case in our family.

Fortune has favoured me in Tori's support for my running. It's a point I reiterate, but it's because I realise how unique and valuable her encouragement is. In many relationships, the runner often faces friction from their partners when they want to dedicate time to running, be it a race or a long training session. It can be challenging for non-runners to grasp why someone would voluntarily run 20 miles for the fun of it.

Tori and the kids are my universe, the absolute core of my existence. They are the reason why my life has meaning. And Tori shares the same sentiment. When we first met in Spain, I was financially well off. It must have appeared to her when we did finally get together that she was joining a life of comfort. However, that wasn't the case. Without delving into the specifics, it was a dramatic shift from riches to rags.

But Tori's loyalty remained unshaken, and our way of life transformed. We focus on creating memories for our children rather than chasing after material wealth. I've learned from my upbringing that happiness doesn't necessarily hinge on financial abundance. The quest for wealth can be overwhelming and unsatisfying, a perpetual cycle of chasing an ever-moving goalpost.

Tori's steadfast support and our decision to live this way is a testament to the value of time. Our way of life might not resonate with everyone, but for us, time is the most precious resource. If you spend your life only working, accumulating possessions without having the time to enjoy them, what's the point? The real key is balance, and while our balance may tip farther away from financial pursuits than others might be comfortable with, I've learned from my mother that one can thrive on little. It's an important lesson I'm determined to pass on to Skye, Summer, and Jackson. While they'll have the freedom to choose their own path, I want them to always know that a fulfilling life isn't necessarily dictated by material wealth but rather by cherishing experiences and connections.

Reflecting on my time in Spain, I could easily succumb to regret, and while I do regret the person I became and the reckless choices I made, I can't overlook the serendipity that brought me to my future wife and the mother of my children.

Odd as it might sound, the vestiges of my former self didn't completely vanish until I stumbled upon running. Up until that point, I still occasionally yearned for nights filled with drugs and alcohol, and my old penchant for the wild remained dormant.

However, fatherhood imposed a necessary change in that regard. I quit drugs and limited my alcohol intake to sporadic indulgences. As my connection with running deepened, the desire to embrace a healthier lifestyle became increasingly compelling. Perhaps my addictive tendencies shifted their focus, but the more I progressed in my running journey, the more I recognised that adopting a healthy lifestyle was pivotal in maximising its benefits. My addiction to pushing limits and seeking new heights didn't vanish; it just found a more productive outlet.

During my previous life, I was driven to be the best, and that same determination fuels my approach to running. Knowing when to say "enough" remains elusive. I'm perpetually scouting for the next challenge, a trait commonly shared by those who transition from addictions to running. The pursuit of highs persists, but comparing myself in photos from before 2015 to now, it's undeniable that the path I've chosen has been the right one.

In that inaugural run back in January 2015, I simply aimed for Tori and me to lead healthier lives. A concrete plan hadn't formed until I stumbled upon Spartathlon. That race furnished me with a trajectory to focus on. True, it might seem absurd to some. Anyone who witnessed me running at the beginning would likely never fathom that I'd enter such a race. Not in a couple of years, not even in my lifetime. Yet, therein lies the essence of why most people never try. They adhere to the widely accepted narrative that age dictates limitations, that once you reach a certain point in life, you can't achieve what you could in your youth. While this holds an element of truth, effort trumps all. Whether you're in your 40s, 50s, or even 60s, as long as you're willing to invest the effort, you can build fitness. When I stumbled upon running, I was in my 30s, and others even older than me have accomplished equal or greater feats of fitness. Consider Steve Way, a man in his 30s, an overweight smoker, who transformed into a Commonwealth Games marathon runner. His story, like others, became a source of inspiration for me. It's a question of why not? If they could achieve it, why not me? The only real question becomes how badly do you want it?

Chapter 6

Battling Doubts and Discovering Resolve

THE GOWER PENINSULA BECKONED VISITORS WITH its tranquil beaches and breathtaking landscapes. For me, it wasn't about relaxation; I had a daunting challenge ahead. I stood at the Gower Peninsula not to unwind, but to embark on a 50-mile run, equivalent to about one-third of the Spartathlon distance. This endeavour served as a litmus test for my ultimate goal. If I could conquer this, the Spartathlon's allure seemed more attainable. If not, perhaps I was overreaching. Regardless, I felt that my running was still on an upward trajectory.

After the 50k race, me, Tori, and the kids headed to Bulgaria for the summer holidays. Amid the sun-drenched days, my running routine persisted. It wasn't training to me; it was the sheer joy of running. Yet, I supplemented this pleasure with in-depth reading on various training techniques. I synthesised the wisdom of renowned coaches, blending their insights into my own training philosophy. I was confident that if I adhered to scientific principles and sidestepped injuries, I'd inch closer to my goals. But 50 miles was an arduous distance, and I understood it was no trifling feat.

Previously, I approached each race with the mindset that if need be, I could walk it. However, with 50 miles, I questioned whether I'd have the time to amble my way to the finish line. If I resorted to a walking too soon, would the ticking clock best me? The only way to know was to run. Returning to the UK in early September, I deemed it prudent to fit in a couple of races prior to the big 50. My times still improved, a natural consequence of consistent training that now encompassed faster sessions. In September, I clocked 10k in 42:01, and after crossing the line, I sensed that there was more speed within me. I aimed to shave those minutes down to 40. A few weeks later, at the Cardiff Half Marathon, I managed 1:34:00. The race remains hazy in my memory, but Tori's elation was vivid. She was astounded by my time and suggested to me that I may have a natural talent for running. Though my time might not have been remarkably fast, her faith bolstered my confidence.

As I stood before the registration for the Gower 50 a week later, a wave of uncertainty engulfed me. Surveying my fellow participants, I couldn't help but feel a pang of inadequacy. My £25 Sports Direct trail shoes, my budget hydration pack off of Ebay (which inconveniently leaked before the race even began), and my two Lucozade bottles filled with water appeared pitiable in comparison to the top-tier running gear others sported. Everyone else seemed to have spent hundreds on top of the range running gear, which had seemed unnecessary to me, but seeing as I was the only one without it, I couldn't help but question myself. What's more, I was worried about getting lost. My map had been waterlogged by the leaking bladder in my pack and was in tatters, and compasses are only really useful if you know how to use them. I didn't. It wasn't the best start, but my morale was boosted by the various snacks I packed ready for the journey. There were pork pies, discos crisps, jelly babies and whatever else I fancied from the shop I'd gone to the day before. At least I wouldn't go hungry.

The moment to bid farewell to Tori and her dad, Nigel, arrived. I didn't want to disappoint them – or myself – by not reaching the finish line. As the race briefing concluded, we set off. October's drizzly weather wasn't too dreadful, though a bit more sunshine would have been ideal. My anxiety ebbed away as the initial miles passed and I exchanged conversations with fellow runners, pausing for snacks when the cravings struck. My eating wasn't dictated by a strict plan; rather, the mental image of Discos crisps or a pork pie drove my consumption.

The rugged course took me by surprise. Endless ups and downs made it challenging to sustain a consistent pace. Yet, until the 20-mile mark, things were going well. However, something shifted around this point. The psychological burden of having run 20 miles and still being far from the halfway mark started playing tricks on me. Expected fatigue and discomfort were creeping in, making each incline seem steeper than the last and even running on flat terrain a Herculean effort. By mile 30, my knees began to hurt – a haunting reminder of my past knee issues that had thwarted my dream of joining the parachute regiment. I found myself limping – a pathetic sight, and to add insult to injury, the next aid station was still a considerable distance away. Panic set in; most of my snacks had been consumed, and the mere thought of covering another mile seemed overwhelming. The weather mirrored my emotional state – dismal.

I gazed out to the sea, my thoughts wandering back to my youth and the myriad of mistakes I'd made. The roads not taken, the people I had let down, and the precarious situations I had tangled myself in swirled in my mind. If I had different knees, would my life have veered down another path? Would I be trudging this cliffside, battling my own limitations? The turmoil broke when thoughts of Tori and the kids emerged. The twists and turns of my life had led me to them. If I didn't complete this race, they'd still be there, unwavering. But I desired to be a positive influence on my children, and Tori seemed to derive joy from my running journey. If I gave up, would the spectre of my old self return? Would the pounds pile back on? Would I descend into unhappiness? How much farther was that elusive aid station?

After what felt like an eternity, a blessed sight emerged: a pub! Enough of this gruelling race – why was I subjecting myself to this? The Railway pub seemed a beacon of refuge and I caved in and entered. I ordered a beer, sank into a seat, and contemplated the warm coziness around me. The thought of abandoning the race began to make sense. But then, as I took a sip of that pint, something stirred within me – a flicker of determination and an echo of the lessons I'd learned through the challenges life had thrown my way. The old me, the one who took the easy way out, was no longer an option. I knew it was time to step back onto that cliff path, to confront my doubts, my pain, and my own limitations. There was a finish line to reach, but even more so, there was a deeper sense of accomplishment to achieve.

But the pub was warm.. I was comfortable. Running was painful.

I rang Tori and asked her to come and pick me up. My race had disintegrated. A mere 15 miles remained, but with my knees in shambles, those miles might as well have stretched to infinity. As I nursed my beer, the warmth of the pub began to thaw my desolation. Time ticked by, and as Tori and Nigel arrived, I hoisted myself up from the sturdy table, my pint just emptied.

"Am I glad to see you!" I huffed, ready to embrace the comfort of the car.

Tori's response threw me off. "What are you talking about?" she retorted.

"I'm finished. My knees are in agony, and I've lost so much time. There's no way I'll finish."

With an unexpected intensity, Tori asked for my pack. "Why?" I questioned.

"Hand it over. The next checkpoint's only 2 miles away. You can make it there."

"But you're here to pick me up!"

"If you still want to quit at that checkpoint, I'll take you home. But quitting now is not an option"

"But... my knees..."

"Come on, Nath, pull yourself together and give me the pack."

I mulled over my refusal, sensing the resolute determination in her eyes. I complied, reluctantly handing over my pack. My goal was simple – to limp my way to that next checkpoint, solidify my exit from the race, and surrender to the inevitable. The thought struck me that the beer had oddly injected me with a burst of energy. Camille Herron, the renowned American ultra-runner, once set a world record while downing beers along the way; perhaps there was a grain of wisdom in that quirky strategy. I was moving – painfully, yes – but I was moving. Before long, the mist revealed a pair of runners behind me. In my memory, they almost appear as knights in shining armour, but in reality, they were just fellow runners.

"Hey mate, how are you feeling?" One of the fellow runners, asked as we hobbled along.

"I've been better," I admitted. "Stopped for a bit at the pub back there, feeling a bit better, but my knees are killing me. I might not carry on past the next checkpoint."

"I'm Nick," he introduced himself, gesturing to his companion. "This is Mark. What's your name?"

"I'm Nathan."

As we exchanged introductions, Mark grinned. "Have you run many 50 milers before?"

"This is my first. Probably my last too," I sighed.

Nick and Mark exchanged a knowing glance, sharing a chuckle. "That's exactly what we thought on our first one," Mark said. "Stick with us. We'll finish together."

Grateful for their encouragement, I managed a smile, though deep down I was still convinced that I would quit within a mile. But fate had other plans; the determination of Tori and the unexpected companionship of Nick and Mark were the undercurrents that carried my aspirations. The simplest acts of kindness and support can steer the course of a life. Chatting with them, I learned that they were both part of the organisation behind the Swansea Half Marathon. Nick, a race founder, and Mark, handling the tech side, were experienced ultra runners who had known moments of doubt similar to mine. Their belief in my potential to finish began to lift my own spirits.

I gazed at them, realising that the very essence of this endeavour lay in those who surrounded me. In their camaraderie, I found the strength to keep moving forward. I was amidst a band of warriors, all striving to conquer their own trials. As we moved through the mist and the rain, the three of us became an unspoken alliance, enduring each step together.

When the checkpoint finally appeared, its welcoming lights cutting through the fog, my knees were still protesting, but my spirit had transformed. I no longer saw an exit; I saw the possibility of moving forward. The prospect of quitting became increasingly distant, and the determination to finish solidified. As I reached the checkpoint, my pace a shadow of what it had been, Tori and Nigel were waiting, expressions of resolute support.

I was on the edge of an internal transformation, a shift from self-doubt to the realisation that challenges and pain were not roadblocks, but catalysts. It wasn't a race against time or fellow runners; it was a race against my own limitations. The physical pain was real, but the mental battle was where the true victory lay. With renewed determination and the support of those who believed in me, I embarked on the remaining miles, no longer defined by my doubts but driven by the unyielding resolve to see this journey through.

Retrieving my pack from Tori, I declared, "I'll see you at the end." It was as if I was the protagonist in a movie, facing a triumphant moment. She grinned, knowing that her support had helped propel me forward.

With about a half-marathon distance left, nothing was certain, but my knees had stabilised. A sharp pain in one of my toes and a throbbing ache in my foot accompanied me, but the companionship of Nick, Mark, and another Nick, a friend of theirs, helped the miles slide by a bit faster. They stayed with me until I was about four miles from the finish line. Knowing that I could hobble the remaining distance within the cut-off time, I encouraged them to go on ahead. The excruciating pain was now a persistent throb, melding with the other aches in my feet. But it wasn't going to deter me.

Hobbling on, step by step, I knew that each stride was a stride toward victory. My thoughts drifted back to that first January run, the painful gasping for breath after just a mile. Now, this was a different kind of pain, but one that encapsulated the essence of ultra-running. I'd been inspired by the book 'Ultramarathon Man' by Dean Karnazes, Dean's experience during the Western States 100 Miler flashed in my mind – his agony reduced him to a crawl, yet he pushed on. I wasn't crawling, not yet, and that meant I could go further. I felt a pang of embarrassment for my despair around mile 30, believing I had to quit. The vantage point of the finish line painted everything in a more positive light.

Those last 4 miles were a stretch of time I can't quite quantify, but as the finish line finally emerged into view, an overwhelming sense of elation surged through me. The pain momentarily faded into the background as I crossed the line. Tori and Nigel's smiles radiated a pride that matched my own sense of accomplishment. The medal that graced my chest held more weight than its physical form – it represented the triumph of overcoming doubt, the power of perseverance, and the indomitable spirit of the journey.

"Aren't you glad you carried on now?" Tori's words resonated as I basked in the glory of the finish line. A simple smile was my reply; it said more than words ever could. I lingered for a while, absorbing the race's atmosphere and reflecting on the journey. Nick and Mark were already indulging in the post-race chili, and I extended my gratitude to them. Little did they know that their kindness and support that day would ripple through my future running endeavours, I will be eternally grateful to them for getting me through that first 50 mile ultra.

I had been on the brink of quitting, but thanks to the two of them and Tori's belief, I persevered. With 50 miles behind me, the realm of possibilities expanded. Could I conquer a 100k? 100 miles? 153 miles? There were no limitations that I could perceive.

Back home, the shower's water felt like a healing balm. Ultra runners know that the best showers follow such races, and this one was transformative. The warm water momentarily eased my aches. Changing into fresh clothes, I felt like I was on top of the world. The sense of achievement from pushing through adversity to reach the finish line was unparalleled. One of my toenails was missing, my knees were in agony, and my feet were screaming, but this was a temporary state. The pizza and beer Nigel offered me tasted heavenly. It was a stark contrast to my earlier solitary beer, which had felt like a remedy for my despair. Now, I felt like a victorious hero. Soon enough, exhaustion pulled me into slumber on the sofa.

So this is what happens when you keep your New Year's resolutions? The experience made me vow to create and stick to new ones every year. Why wouldn't everyone? The general consensus would have deemed the idea of covering 50 miles by October from a non-runner's starting point in January a fool's errand, if not downright unadvisable. Yet, I had shattered those misconceptions through dedication, determination and sheer effort. The journey had transformed me into a person I was proud of, someone my kids would someday look up to. Despite the fatigue that often shadowed my days, and the moments of doubt during tough runs, I was seeing results. I had shed a significant amount of weight – perhaps too much in some eyes. People I hadn't seen in a while wondered where the rest of me had gone and I heard people ask Tori "Is he ok?" and "he's looking ill". My mum was concerned, but I reassured her that I was eating healthily and training hard. While nutrition would become a more focused aspect later, at that moment I knew I had found my passion. Running was changing my life.

Belief was the cornerstone. The improvements I had witnessed only steeled my resolve to keep pushing. What would 2016 bring? The sky truly felt like the limit. My theory was that belief got you three quarters of the way there; the rest is down to hard work and dedication. Nothing too complex.

Chapter 7:

Embracing Challenges

HALF AN HOUR HAD SLIPPED BY IN THE CAR, AND I found myself battling not just external doubt, but the inner struggle that had a way of holding me back. Why was I always my own obstacle?

The notion of joining a running club hadn't thrilled Tori at first. Perhaps a shadow of uncertainty lingered within her, wondering if my newfound passion for running might compromise our family life. It wasn't the case. My intention was purely to find and meet like-minded individuals who shared my passion, and hopefully improve my running. Yet, here I was, grappling with my own hesitations, unable to make the simple decision to step out of the car and join the running club. Was I out of my depth? This was a running club with real runners.

The first night at 3M Gorseinon Road Runners had been almost a missed opportunity. Nearly giving in to the temptation to drive back home, I ultimately took a deep breath and forced myself to step out of the car. The night was chilly, but I summoned the courage to jog over to the nearest runner I saw, who turned out to be Paul Harris, the club secretary I had chatted with earlier over email.

Paul inquired about my race times. I shared that I was nearing 40 minutes for a 10k and 1 hour 30 minutes for a half-marathon. My primary goal was to improve my performance in ultras.

"We've got another ultra runner among us," Paul grinned. "I'm signed up for MDS in a few months."

MDS, the Marathon Des Sables, a 6-day race through the Sahara Desert, often touted as one of the toughest races on Earth, a view not universally shared by all ultra enthusiasts. The entry fee of around 3,000 pounds could deter some, but the allure of the experience was undeniable.

Paul's encouraging words resonated with me, "You'll definitely get quicker if you keep running with us. There are some really fast guys here." The idea of surrounding myself with runners of all levels, including those much faster than me, piqued my curiosity. Maybe this was a leap I needed to take.

Being part of the running club had an unexpected positive side effect – I had a group of people to engage in running discussions with. Tori probably appreciated the relief from my relentless running talk. Moreover, I discovered that my substantial weight loss after taking up running wasn't as unique as I thought. Paul and several other club members had also experienced significant weight loss, so my transformation became less a spectacle and more of a shared achievement.

My inaugural year at the club was filled with surprises. I received the 'Newcomer of the Year' and 'Club Runner of the Year' awards, and I even secured the top runner in the league championship for our club races. Winning seven races out of seven entered had made an impression, showcasing a competitive spirit that I didn't know existed. As I engaged in friendly rivalry with my fellow club members, I found my times for shorter races steadily improving. My hard work led to a time of 36:15 for the Eastleigh 10k, and I finally broke the 1 hour 30 minutes barrier for the half-marathon roughly a year after I had started running.

I thought about running the downhill mile that had been such a challenge on January 1st of the previous year, just to gauge my progress, but another idea began to take shape. Why not run from Swansea to Manchester in time for the Manchester United versus Swansea City match on January 2nd? This plan combined two of my passions – running and football. Tori kindly agreed to act as the support car driver, meeting me at various points along the 187-mile route. The adventure was on. Although the distance was comparable to Spartathlon, I had five days for this journey compared to 36 hours in the Greek ultramarathon.

The weather conditions in Greece during Spartathlon differed vastly from the cold and rainy climate of Wales and North-West England at the start of the year. Rain accompanied me for the initial days, almost like a faithful companion. The constant downpour triggered flood warnings along my route, and at times, I questioned my decision. Yet, as the adventure unfolded, I found solace in the journey itself. The lack of a direct race against time allowed me to embrace the road, the rain, and the sheer experience of it all. I felt alive.

I had envisioned running around the perimeter of Old Trafford's pitch upon arrival. Although safety and security would prevent that from happening, I was featured in the club's match day program, I'll take that!. I managed to reach the stadium a few hours before kick-off, had enough time for a celebratory beer and settled to watch the game, United were 2-1 winners. A great day. I raised some money for charity, which helped me to keep going during the worst of the weather, and just a few days after I finished there were some pretty nasty floods in Manchester, they really did follow me the whole way. I could have been a lot less lucky with the weather, even though it may not have felt like it at the time.

The five consecutive days of high mileage from my run to Manchester hadn't drained me as much as I expected. Soon, my focus shifted to the upcoming Vale of Glamorgan Coastal Ultra on April 2nd. While I wasn't aiming to win, I was confident I could complete the race.

When the day came round I was worried about getting lost, and so I thought I'd just wait and see who was running a pace that felt comfortable to me and try to stick with them. As it happened I got chatting to Matthew Ryan around 4 miles in and without really meaning to we ended up running over 20 miles together, although he did let slip that he knew the route, so it would have been hard for him to get rid of me. He has since become a good friend, I enjoyed our time running together that day. It would have been nice to finish together but he was starting to struggle with around five miles to go and told me to go on ahead. I would have been happy to stick with him, but he insisted, if you're having a low patch it can add to your stress if you know you're slowing someone else down too. I carried on and caught up with another runner, Sam, we crossed the line together in joint 5th place.

There was something different about my mindset at the end of this run. I knew that if I'd been familiar with the route and I'd had the confidence to try and stay with the leaders from the start I could have made the podium, perhaps I may have won. Thoughts of having a good go at my next race crossed my mind, I was entered into the Ham & Lyme 100k down in Somerset a few months later, It was a fairly low-key race and the winning time from the year before seemed achievable, so I felt like perhaps 1st place was a possibility, was I getting carried away, was it belief or simply over confidence? What was a thought in the back of my mind at that point got louder and louder the closer it got to race day in July.

The day after Vale of Glamorgan there was a 20 mile race close to home. The route went through Tumble, the village where I grew up, so I wanted to give it a go. I knew from the Swansea to Manchester run that I'd be ok running long on back-to-back days. But the Manchester run had been at a very leisurely pace. These were races, I blew up after 15 miles, reduced to a walk. I still hadn't figured out how to fuel properly during these long runs, I was winging it. Nowadays I always try to make sure my nutrition's on point – I have to, fuelling is key in these longer races. Getting the fuelling and hydration wrong will derail all that hard work we put into training,

Before the Swansea to Manchester run I had managed to fit in a couple of marathons. The Black Mountain Trail Marathon in the Brecon Beacons was very hilly, and a lot more gruelling than the Portsmouth Coastal Marathon a few weeks later, which was full of festive cheer. There were mince pies and beers at the water stations, and all considered I was really pleased with my time of 3:38. I hit the wall 18 miles in, and the last 8 were a bit of a slog. I would return to Portsmouth a year later and finish in the top 10.

As I approached the Ham & Lyme 100k, I strategically scheduled several marathons, setting my sights on a sub-3-hour finish at the upcoming Manchester Marathon in the spring. Aiming for such a feat within a little over a year of starting my running journey may have been a little audacious, but it all came down to the combination of belief and hard work. I delved into the science of effective training methods, and maintained my unwavering belief in what I might be able to achieve.

Aside from my family, running was now the biggest thing in my life, and as with most things in life you get out what you put in. I understood that achieving a sub-3-hour marathon wouldn't come from occasional jogs or mere hope; but train smart over a consistent period of time and it's amazing how quickly things can progress.

As I strode forward on this journey, I was continually surprised at how dedicated training coupled with a little self belief could lead to exponential improvements. The ultimate lesson was clear: whether it's in running or any other aspect of life, a combination of persistence, knowledge, and confidence can drive us beyond our perceived limits.

And so, with every stride and every race, I continued to push the boundaries, always setting my sights on new goals and exciting challenges.

Chapter 8

Triumph and Tribulations

THE DAY OF THE MANCHESTER MARATHON ARRIVED, and I stood on the start line, a mix of determination and uncertainty coursing through me. The sub-3-hour marathon – a 6-minute and 50-second per mile pace – was the ambitious target I'd set for myself. While I knew I could maintain this pace for a considerable stretch, I was embarking on uncharted territory – a full marathon at this pace was a monumental challenge for me.

The city of Manchester, so deeply intertwined with my life, offered a familiar backdrop to this audacious endeavour. With its electrifying atmosphere and personal connections, the day was set to be memorable regardless of the outcome. As the race started, I found myself in that magical rhythm where each stride felt perfect, every breath invigorating. I could sense the energy of the crowd propelling me forward, my legs moving to the rhythm of the city itself.

The miles seemed to melt beneath my feet. My pace, steady and comfortable, carried me through the urban landscape, the cheering spectators lined on each side of the roads adding to my momentum. The support from my family, especially Tori and Skye, who were hopping on and off the train at various points along the route fuelled my determination. The 18 mile mark came, then the 20, then the 22 and the elusive wall stayed at bay. When I hit the finishing straight with 2:58 on the clock I was overcome with emotion. I'm not usually one to cry over my own achievements, and so it's a little baffling why it happened then. I guess it was just the whole atmosphere of the day, the fact I'd run a sub 3 hour marathon, I'd achieved the goal I had set out to achieve.

Tori and Skye met me at the finish, I suggested heading to the pub for a celebratory drink. After a couple of drinks I needed a wee. As I replayed a montage of memories from the race in my head I happened to look down and noticed my pee was red; Manchester United red. Perhaps fitting for the occasion, but was also quite alarming. I knew that wasn't meant to happen, and I went back to the table outside, mentioning it to Tori.

"That doesn't sound good. Do you feel Ok?" she said, obviously with a little concern in her voice.

"Actually, no," I replied, "I think I'm gonna be sick."

A wave of queasiness had hit me. I tried to get up to go back to the bathroom but then felt like I'd been knocked over. I was on the floor in a pool of sweat. The stuff was just pouring off me, like I'd never known before. Tori said I'd hit the ground in a wave of slow motion and I passed out for a few seconds, but all I remember is the sweat. It was literally forming a puddle around me on the floor.

A couple of paramedics arrived and checked me over. After a while I began to feel better, and figured that if the paramedics hadn't rushed me to hospital I was probably Ok. No need to get dramatic about the whole thing, if anything I felt more embarrassed. All the same though poor Skye looked terrified and had been crying through the whole ordeal, afterwards she had blurted out "I thought you were going to die daddy!". I was haunted by the image of her frightened little face during races for a while afterwards. I vowed to take it a little easier in the next couple of races.

We went back to Tori's parents for the rest of the day and I just relaxed. The whole thing played on my mind, and I went to see a doctor the following week. He gave me a check-up and said everything seemed fine. His theory was that I had fainted after seeing the blood in my pee and that, coupled with the low blood pressure after the exertion of the marathon, made me feel queasy. I thought he was probably right but was under strict orders from Tori to not push too hard if I was to go ahead with the next couple of marathons. Someone else might have tried to forbid me from doing them, but she trusted me to know what I could and couldn't handle. I did go through with the Great Welsh and Blackpool Marathons and paced them a little easier than Manchester, finishing them in 3:05 and 3:06. I have since had quite a few episodes of bloody urine, usually in the heat when I'm dehydrated, some of the hardier old school Bulgarian runners I sometimes train with tell me in their hoarse toned broken English "Nathan, don't worry, this is just weakness leaving your body!"

The incident at the Manchester Marathon lingered in my mind, like a shadow cast over the thrill of triumph. These experiences transformed my perspective on setbacks and physical vulnerability, reshaping my understanding of both the human body's endurance and its fragility.

As my miles grew lighter for a while, I engaged in conversations with fellow runners at the club. Among them was Richard Webster, a club founder and accomplished marathoner from an earlier era. His wisdom served as a compass and I'd often turn to Richard for some advice, his advice to back off a little bit guided me to reevaluate my approach. Tori's maternal watch was ticking and the counsel of seasoned runners' advice pointed to a lesson I was learning – the need to balance ambition with self-care and family.

The subsequent weeks became a period of recalibration, a time to rebuild my body's reserves and rekindle the fire of anticipation. I took to the quiet trails, savouring each step, and allowing myself to savour the beauty of my surroundings.

My return to racing, timed for the end of May, held a different flavour. Each race became an opportunity to apply the lessons I had gathered. In this period of reflection and recovery, I continued to train with focus but also with a deepened understanding that strength isn't solely about the pace of one's strides, but also about the wisdom in knowing when to slow down.

The break rekindled my spirit and paved the way for a fresh challenge, the Edinburgh Marathon. Armed with a renewed sense of vigour, I found myself standing at the starting line with a determined goal: to set a new personal best. As I had progressively shed the lingering shadows of Manchester, I had come to recognise the fine line between confidence and overconfidence.

The notion of aiming for a 2:45 marathon time felt audacious, but I felt that I had the capacity to push myself further. The race commenced, I felt good but I would soon realise that I had set a pace that was unsustainable and I started to slow. My body reminding me that even ambitious goals require a realistic execution. I crossed the finish line in 2:52. A new personal best. What's more I didn't faint, pee blood or even excessively sweat after I'd finished so all was good.

The triumphs of that day weren't mine alone; my family, led by Tori and joined by Skye, shared in the marathon spirit. Tori and Skye ran their first races that weekend too – as part of the 'Edinburgh Marathon Festival' there are a number of shorter races. Tori ran 10k and Skye ran 2k. The gloss was taken off my success by the fact that Skye took a tumble at the start of her race and was trampled over by some of the other kids as they pushed forward when the gun went off. She picked herself up, bloody faced and scratched from the gravel and continued the race. She cried most of the way but her determination to finish still inspires me to this day – I was unbelievably proud but heartbroken at the same time. Nothing a huge Mr Whippy ice cream wouldn't sort out though, she still remembers that ice cream to this day. Sadly Skye has lost interest in running as she's gotten older, but Summer really enjoys it, I'll often get back from a training run to find Summer lacing up her shoes and wanting to join me for the cooldown.

As my marathon times improved, I faced a crossroads. The temptation to chase faster times at the marathon was undeniable, but the allure of the ultras pulled me in another direction. I recognised that to truly thrive in the world of ultras, I needed to tailor my training differently – focused on endurance, running for longer rather than faster. So, I decided to focus on the ultras, but there was a little something to fit in on the way home first.

Summer and Jackson had been staying with Tori's parents, and so we picked them up on the way back from Edinburgh. Skye was able to show off her battle scars while I started to get prepared for my next challenge. I'd been looking at a website for the records on UK peaks a while before, and thought the Welsh 3 Peaks record seemed pretty achievable. Running a fast marathon and then having my legs seize up on a long car journey probably wasn't the best preparation, but seeing as we were going past the mountains anyway I thought I might as well have a go. The record involves the fastest possible time for reaching the peaks of Snowdon, Cadair Idris and Pen Y Fan, including the time taken to drive between them. Looking back now I was woefully unprepared. I had never been on any of these peaks before so I didn't know the routes, and we didn't really know the way between them so would have to navigate on the way. My legs were pretty wrecked, but I figured I wouldn't be running too fast on the way up anyway and could just let the slopes help on the way down as long as I could stay on my feet.

With these thoughts in mind, I embarked on a new challenge, a journey not defined by a finish line but rather by the experience itself.

Snowdon, Cadair Idris, and Pen Y Fan – these peaks were no strangers to avid climbers and nature enthusiasts. But for me, they represented a realm of unexplored terrain. Despite my weary legs and a journey that likely sabotaged the prospects of peak performance, I embarked on this last minute mission.

Tori and the girls formed the support crew at the foot of each peak. With Jackson, just 11 weeks old, nestled among them. I must admit I was relieved to have got the last one, Pen Y Fan, finished. It was a tough day, and I couldn't wait to rest afterwards. My time was 9 hours, 6 minutes. Apparently the routes I took were actually the longest ones, and we had bad luck with the driving in between. We got lost, we got stuck behind tractors, we couldn't find anywhere to park for a while... The record has since been broken by my friend Matthew Ryan, who I'd run most of the Vale Coastal Ultra with. I knew it would go and I knew that someone would take a good chunk of time off it, I'm pleased he did it. I'd like to go back and have another go. Maybe some day.

As my legs found solace in rest and my thoughts turned to the future, I held in my heart the dreams of yet more uncharted paths and new challenges waiting to be embraced.

The weeks leading up to the Ham & Lyme 100k buzzed with anticipation, there were around six weeks between that crazy weekend and my target race. I was feeling a surge of confidence leading up to the race and conversations with fellow club mates spurred me on further with comments like "you could win that 100k mate" and "you should try and win that race, what have you got to lose". The marathon times I had run in the spring and the Welsh 3 Peaks record had given me the confidence to know that the distance wouldn't break me. As for winning it, it would all depend on who else I would have to beat. There may well have been others who had seen the modest winning time the year before and planned to try and beat it. I didn't know any of the other runners who would be racing.

Though I was transforming, I remained conscious of my inexperience – I still didn't feel like I was a fast runner; my times at the marathons hadn't put me anywhere near 1st place, and I was just running at a pace I felt like I could sustain through my training. I knew that for 100k I wouldn't be running fast at the beginning and would only consider it if I had to try and put the hammer down towards the end. Would I even be able to push harder after running that far? I have to admit I couldn't help but look beyond Ham & Lyme a little bit too. Spartathlon didn't seem as far off as it once had, all those months ago. I started to research the qualifying times with a little more interest and thought they might be just about within my capabilities. Later in the year I would put everything into trying to achieve that. For now though I had a race to try and win.

Chapter 9:

Could I really win an ultra?

AS I STOOD IN THE DESERTED CAR PARK OVERLOOKING the sea, waiting for the toilet block to be unlocked, I felt something I had never felt at a race before. Nerves. Not just the average nerves about whether or not I might finish, but something altogether more intense. I played down my hopes of victory when I spoke to Tori, I always do. I was glad to have her with me; we decided it would be too long a day for the kids, I could be out there all day, so Tori's parents were looking after them for the weekend, and we had booked a hotel nearby.

I knew very little about the course, except that apparently a lot of people had got lost the year before. This terrified me. My map-reading skills were pretty much non-existent, and I didn't own a fancy watch, or have the know-how to load the route onto the one I'd borrowed from a club mate. My plan was to run within view of people for as long as I could and hope that I could find a burst of energy towards the end so I could put a gap on whoever was near me. As the other runners started to arrive, I tried to spot who the main competitors would be, but it was hard to tell. I figured I'd just try to follow whoever was up front early on and hope they knew the way better than I did.

My heart rate was raised a little bit because of the adrenalin, but luckily my stomach was perfectly settled. I'd devoured a Frankie and Benny's spaghetti dinner with pizza bread the night before, which I hoped would give me the energy for the early miles, then I'd take advantage of the picnic aid stations that had been promised along the way. The car park had filled up and before I knew it. Dave the race director called everyone over for the pre race briefing. He cracked a couple of bad jokes that helped ease the nerves and explained a couple of route diversions, I hoped the person I'd be following was taking it all in.

When Dave gave the starting signal (A fake phone call from world famous ultra runner Killian Jornet) which amused half the field and confused the rest, we took off down hill. It seemed clear after a while who the front runners were going to be, I pushed to stick with them. After the initial few miles I found a steady pace and got chatting to some of the other guys, it seemed like there were a few who were hoping to win. One was Dan Masters, who would later become a friend I would see at a number of races, and who would go on to win The UK's Grand Slam of 100 milers later on. Another was a guy called Allen, who I would end up running a lot with that day. The other guy who seemed in with a shot of the win was Lee, and the four of us took turns leading, forming an unspoken alliance as we navigated the route together. The course stretched ahead, winding through the landscape. I didn't know these men, their stories or backgrounds, but our shared pursuit united us.

I was determined to make the most of the aid stations, a strategy that differed from some of the other runners. Lee especially was in and out in a few moments, but I took a couple of minutes at each one when it came, chatted a little bit to the volunteers and savoured some cake or fruit, or whatever treats were on offer. As I approached the last aid station before the halfway mark, I couldn't believe it when I was handed a glass of Pimm's! I hadn't anticipated enjoying something like this during a race, but with the adrenaline and excitement, I thought, "Why not?" It tasted surprisingly good.

Throughout the first half, we encountered runners going in the opposite direction – the 50k participants starting from what would become our halfway point. Encouragement flowed freely as we exchanged high fives and cheers. The camaraderie was infectious, although occasionally you'd come across a more focused runner who kept their head down. But these were exceptions; for the most part, everyone was incredibly friendly.

The initial nerves had faded, and I found myself chatting a lot with Allen. We seemed to be in sync, running at a similar pace. It felt like I had gained a new running companion. However, Allen started having some trouble just after the halfway point.

"I'm not sure what's going on, but I think I might have had a reaction to something," he said, his breathing a bit more laboured.

"Can you make it to the next aid station?" I inquired, concerned. "The medic there can check you over."

"I should be okay," he replied, though it was clear he was struggling.

Dan had surged ahead some time ago, and as I fretted over Allen's well-being, another worry began to creep in – how much distance Dan was putting between us. He was an obviously fit guy, with muscles upon muscles, and I began to wonder if we'd even catch sight of him again. Lee had disappeared from my view, and Allen seemed to be giving it all he had. For all I knew, another contender might be making their way through the field. So, as we tackled the final climb toward Ham Hill Country Park – part of the "Ham" in "Ham & Lyme" – Dan's figure came into view just ahead, I felt a surge of relief. The three of us reached the aid station nearly in unison. Tori, observing this spectacle, seemed amazed to see me.

"Nath, you're leading!" Tori's surprised voice rang out. "How are you feeling?"

"Actually, really good," I grinned. "But Allen's struggling. Would you mind staying with him for a while and make sure the medics check him over?"

"Of course."

With a quick nod to Tori, I extended my gratitude to the aid station volunteers, engaging in some light conversation as I nibbled on choice snacks from the spread. These volunteers were Dave the race director's parents, I learned, embodying the welcoming spirit that seemed to infuse the entire event. The friendly chats, the nourishment, and the picturesque surroundings often made me forget I was in a race.

"Are you going to be okay, Allen?" I inquired, feeling torn about leaving him behind.

"Yeah, mate. Don't worry," he reassured me. "I've had a reaction to some Hogweed, I think. My son's going to run with me and make sure I'm alright."

"I'll wait until he gets here," Tori interjected. "I'll catch up with you later on. Go for it, Nath!"

Her genuine excitement fuelled my determination, and I knew that she would make sure Allen was ok. I had initially considered sticking with Allen for a good portion of the race, but his situation had altered my plans. While Allen's misfortune had tempered my spirits, the main concern was still making sure I didn't lose my way during the return journey to Lyme Regis. Dan was preparing to depart, a signal that it was time to focus and continue the race.

Dan and I maintained a similar pace, capitalising on the long downhill stretch that mirrored the earlier ascent. Our progress was soon joined by Lee, who had seemingly experienced a sudden resurgence. As we approached the next aid station, I could sense that Dan was grappling with fatigue. Feeling strong, I pressed on without slowing, while Lee matched my pace closely.

"Do you know the way?" I asked Lee.

"Oh yeah, I'm local. I know this route well," he said confidently.

His familiarity with the route was precisely what I needed. With Lee leading, I felt reassured that I wouldn't lose my way on the homestretch. As we ran side by side, we exchanged a few words. The topic of my relatively short time in the running world emerged, and Lee was astounded. He had years of running experience, yet my rapid progress was an anomaly to him. Reflecting on this now, I realise my positive mindset played a crucial role. Belief, I think, is what often hinders people from reaching their full potential. Tori's admiration for my achievements fuelled my ambition, and I believed that consistent effort would translate to continuous improvement.

Now, sharing the lead with Lee, my competitive side kicked in and I began to wonder how I would emerge victorious. He was equally driven to win, and considering his second-place finish the previous year, I knew he wouldn't relinquish the lead easily. Dan had fallen behind, making it clear that the battle for first place was primarily between myself and Lee. The penultimate aid station, perched high on a misty hill, offered a moment of respite. The fog obscured any view of the sea and the finish line, which was supposed to be visible on clear days. Lee ran straight through grabbing a water on the way whilst I stopped for a moment for a quick bite and chatted with the volunteers once more, I tried not to stay too long at the aid station and was amazed at how good I felt. The weariness of covering such a distance was undeniable, yet I felt confident that I could catch up to Lee without overexerting myself.

With determination burning in my chest, I pressed onward, the final leg of the race beckoning me to reach for the finish line and the prospect of victory.

Soon, Lee emerged just ahead of me on the trail. As I closed the gap, I detected a shift in the air between us. Until that point, our conversation had flowed naturally, like a friendly training run. But now, when I attempted to engage, the responses were terse. I pondered whether fatigue had silenced him. However, I gradually realised, unfamiliar with leading, that a heightened competitive instinct had surged as the finish drew near. The camaraderie transformed into focused determination on both our parts. The rapid change in dynamic struck me as odd initially. But as we drew closer to the end, I too became more attuned to the competitive spirit. I contemplated when I should execute my decisive move. Our pace remained steady. Knowing I had to avoid relying on a sprint finish for victory, I began to think how best to make my move.

With one final aid station before the finish, I observed Lee's struggle once we had passed it. It was time to make my move. Though silent, my mental message was clear: legs, run faster. They responded, and I felt myself surge ahead, alone. The last miles lay ahead, and I pushed myself further. My breathing quickened, warmth radiating through my body. Could I maintain this pace? Would Lee find a burst of energy at the end? I pictured him trailing closely, even though a glance revealed he was not. A new sensation swept over me – a touch of apprehension. It was the first time outside of the club races that I had raced while chasing a specific position, and the gravity of it weighed heavily for a moment.

Approaching the edge of the town, my worst fear materialised. I was disoriented, lost in a labyrinth of streets. The route, etched on an OS map in my backpack, was useless in my hands. Consulting it would only have Lee passing me. Panic seized me, and I began asking anyone I encountered for directions to the seafront. I darted through the streets of Lyme Regis, fearing that Lee had seized the opportunity to overtake while I ran in circles. The impending loss of victory seemed inevitable. The thought that I had come so close to winning only for it to slip away gnawed at me.

Amid the panic, a clock tower, mentioned earlier as a landmark near the finish, came into view. A volunteer in a high-visibility vest directed me onto a path. Summoning every ounce of energy, I surged forward, my legs propelling me into a final sprint. The applause and cheers grew louder, a crescendo of encouragement. Had victory slipped from my grasp? Or was this truly my moment? Just the thought brought an irrepressible grin to my face, a memory etched in Tori's mind.

The final corner emerged, the finish sign in sight. Applause and Tori's radiant smile greeted me as I sprinted toward the finish line.

"Did I win?" I managed to ask, my breath still ragged from the final sprint.

"Yes, you won," Tori replied, her smile illuminating the moment. She must have said more, but my joy in achieving what I had set out for eclipsed everything else.

A medal was placed around my neck, and the race directors, Dave and Natanya, handed me the winners trophy. It was surreal, a feeling of accomplishment that I had never experienced.

"Is this your first win?" Dave inquired.

"In this kind of race, yes. I've won a few club races before but nothing this long," I replied, still absorbing the reality of the moment.

"Congratulations, well done! By the way, did you know that you shattered the course record by about 2 hours?"

The notion of a course record hadn't even crossed my mind; it was a concept foreign to me. Just minutes later, Lee crossed the finish line and offered his congratulations. I sensed the mixed emotions he must have felt, securing 2nd place by only a couple of minutes for two consecutive years. He did eventually claim his victory at the same race the following year.

I stayed a little while after the race to cheer the other runners in, but it wasn't long before the lure of fish & chips became too strong, so I thanked everyone for a great day and made my way back to the car with Tori. The car park was up a steep hill, and this was when my legs really started to complain. I was ok though, I liked the feeling, I was on such a high from the race, but I was definitely glad to get to the top.

The taste of fish and chips was a reward in itself, each bite infused with the satisfaction of victory. I recounted the highlights of the race to Tori as we ate, and her excitement matched mine. Her constant support never ceased to amaze me; some of my running friends would express disbelief at the harmony we shared in this aspect of my life.

"You wouldn't believe the grief I get over my running!" some would exclaim.

"Really?" I would respond, genuinely puzzled. "It's just running."

I struggled to comprehend the negativity. There are surely worse hobbies or pursuits a partner could be engaged in. Of course, if running cut into family time, it could be problematic, but I carefully planned my training to avoid such conflicts. Early mornings and late evenings were when I made time for runs, ensuring that my family's routines remained uninterrupted. I involved my family in my races – my kids took joy in cheering me on and participating in the shorter kids races. For Tori, it was simple: she just wanted to see me happy.

Upon returning to the hotel, the effort of getting out of the car was surprisingly challenging. It was a stark reminder of the distance I had covered. The irony was obvious; throughout the race, I had felt comfortable, but now that I had ceased running, the full impact hit my legs like a tidal wave. I mustered determination and gradually managed to stand up, hobbling to our room with every bit of energy I had left. As soon as we got in and I could relax the euphoria of the day returned. I'd won the race, and that accomplishment was a source of pride. Yet, it was more than that – the entire atmosphere of the day etched itself into my memory. The camaraderie I shared with fellow runners, the thundering applause at the finish line, the selflessness of the volunteers who manned the aid stations – all of these impressions swirled in my mind. But beneath it all, a quiet voice persisted and was growing stronger. 100 miles. Could I run a hundred miles? Could that be my next challenge?.

Chapter 10

Who is this guy?

THE ENERGY OF THE DAY HAD SHIFTED AS THE RACE director, Ronnie Staton, fumbled to search my name on Google. News of my 100k victory hadn't circulated like wildfire in the ultra running scene; I was an unfamiliar face in this world. Ronnie's sudden interest was fuelled by his assumption that I, like many first-time 100-mile runners, had started at an unsustainable pace that would inevitably lead to my downfall. And in a sense, he was right – I had pushed hard at the start, although I managed to hang on much longer than anticipated. As the race progressed, I was still leading. And maybe, just maybe, Ronnie was allowing himself to consider the possibility that I could actually clinch this race.

Tori remained uncharacteristically quiet, likely relishing the attention being paid to the leader's wife. She had a keen understanding of my goals and although biased she knew how determined I was, She became both curious and amused to witness the dawning realisation among others, who initially doubted my capabilities. It's a funny trait of hers, always believing the impossible is achievable especially in me, even when the odds seem insurmountable she has a way of making you believe you are capable of anything.

The Robin Hood 100 Miler, was an unassuming event with a relatively flat course – ideal conditions for maintaining a consistent pace. My target was to complete it within 16 hours, just below the calculated Spartathlon qualifying time. To achieve this, I needed to average around 9 minutes and 30 seconds per mile. I set off at a pace of 7 minutes and 45 seconds per mile, a pace I knew I could comfortably sustain for a while.

Within the first mile, I surged ahead to take the lead. Everything unfolded as planned until I encountered a setback around the 30-mile mark. I veered off course after missing the marking tape, losing precious time. Although this cost me around 30 minutes, my confidence remained unshaken; I still felt strong. It was around the 60-mile point when Ronnie began his detective work on me. At this point, I felt like I was on my way to securing my spot at the Spartathlon starting line – I only needed to finish, and my pace seemed sufficient. However, 20 miles later, a different reality set in. The 80-mile mark, as many ultra runners will tell you, is where things start to get serious in a 100-mile race. You're tantalisingly close to the finish line, and thoughts of "I can take it easy now, almost there" begin to infiltrate your mind. But just when complacency threatens to creep in, your body reminds you of the miles covered and the fatigue starts to weigh heavily. It was as though a switch had been flicked in my body, sapping my energy and replacing it with a heavy lethargy.

In addition to battling my own physical weariness, I was acutely aware of the relentless pursuit of Alistair Higgins. Alistair, over from Ireland and also chasing Spartathlon qualification, was hot on my heels. His reputation as a formidable runner, with a string of 100 mile victories that year, added an extra layer of pressure. The glow of triumph I had basked in earlier was now dimmed by creeping negativity. The canal path leading towards the finish was supposed to be a triumphant glide, yet my steps felt laboured and sluggish, far from the triumphant sprint I had imagined. With each stride, I told myself, "One foot in front of the other, Nath, just keep moving." But what seemed like a manageable distance during moments of strength now felt insurmountable, a relentless battle.

Five miles to go, the imaginary Gestapo officer I described at the beginning of the book was chasing, I felt his ominous presence. Though it was nothing more than a product of my exhausted mind, the sensation propelled me forward with a burst of energy. I turned around, shielding my head torch, to catch a glimpse of Alistair. He wasn't far behind, likely less than a mile. My desperation drove me to ask Tori, "Are they still following me?" In that moment, the line between reality and my weary mind's concoctions blurred further.

Struggling but resolute, I rounded a corner and saw Ronnie. A surge of hope ignited within me; the finish line must be close. And then, the sight of Tori. "You've done it, Nath," she encouraged. A renewed determination coursed through me, pushing my body into a final sprint. Tori joined me, running by my side, and Ronnie guided us to the finish. As my feet pounded the path, it became clear – this was victory, my second ultra win. The finish line loomed, and I could almost feel the tape breaking across my chest.

But even as triumph painted the moment, an undeniable reality persisted. My dream of qualifying for the ultimate race, Spartathlon, still eluded me. As I crossed the finish line, the wave of accomplishment was tinged with a sense of bittersweetness. My time, although decent, was not swift enough to secure my entry into the coveted Spartathlon.

The taste of victory mingled with the sting of missed opportunity on the journey home made my mind replay every twist and turn of the race, dissecting every moment that could have led to a different outcome. The missed tape, that half-hour detour – how could such a small detail carry such a weight of consequence? 16 hours and 34 minutes for a first 100-miler was no small feat, yet it fell agonisingly short of securing my entry into Spartathlon.

The trip home was a battle between gratitude for what I had achieved and the bitter taste of "almost." I questioned my choices, my training, and the turns of fate that had conspired to keep me just out of reach. The doubts swirled like restless ghosts in my mind. Was I truly capable of Spartathlon? Could I put myself through another agonising 100 miles to try again Or was I merely entertaining a delusion? The proximity of my dream had only heightened the uncertainty. I was so close – dangerously close – to reaching that pinnacle, yet I still stood on the other side of the threshold.

Tori's cheerful reminder of my dual victories brought a smile to my face, a feeble attempt to mask my internal struggle. The days that followed the race carried the weight of introspection. Each thought and contemplation was a step towards embracing the larger narrative – this wasn't just about the final destination, it was about the journey itself. I found a bit of solace in the fact that I had come this far, that I had stood on the brink of triumph, even if I hadn't fully crossed that line.

Weeks turned into months, and the Flitch Way 100k loomed on the horizon, a chance for redemption. The echo of that missed opportunity spurred me on. Doubts lingered like shadows, but I was resolute. I focused on my training, knowing that preparation was the key to unlocking my potential. Could I recover in time? Could I channel my disappointment into determination? The uncertainty was thick, but so was my resolve.

As the calendar marched forward, my mindset shifted. The Spartan spirit that had carried me through countless miles of training and races resurfaced. My eyes were fixed on the future, on the challenge that awaited, and the possibility of turning "almost" into "absolutely." The Flitch Way 100k became more than just a race – it was a second chance, an opportunity to prove that I was more than the sum of my doubts and setbacks.

I delved into research about Spartathlon once more, devouring every piece of information I could find. As I scoured the British Spartathlon Team Facebook page, a thread caught my eye. One comment stood out: "The qualifying time of sub 16:50...." My heart skipped a beat. Could it be? Could I have miscalculated? I fired off a message to the commenter, desperately seeking confirmation. My heart raced as I awaited a response.

The message arrived, bearing news that I could hardly believe. The qualifying time for Spartathlon was not the elusive sub-16 hours and 30 minutes as I had believed – it was sub-16 hours and 50 minutes. I needed to hear it again, this time from another source. And then another, and another. The reality began to sink in. I had already met the qualifying time during the Robin Hood 100 Miler. The despair and frustration that had been gnawing at me was replaced by a surge of pure elation and the winning feeling felt at the end of both the Ham & Lyme and Robin Hood came flooding back! I'd done it!

I was dumbfounded by the realisation. The calculations that had haunted my thoughts for months were, in fact, unnecessary. I had already accomplished what I had set out to do. My dream of participating in Spartathlon was within reach, and the path was clearer than ever before. Entries were opening soon, and I was now secure in the knowledge that my spot was guaranteed. I was going to be on that start line!

The road ahead was no less challenging, but my spirit was renewed. The Flitch Way 100k was now not an opportunity for redemption but a celebration of my success. I trained with newfound vigour, embracing the knowledge that I was capable, that I had already defied my doubts. Some doubt still lurked in the corners of my mind, but the finish line of the Flitch Way 100k was no longer a threshold to cross; it was a gateway to a future I had earned. I went on to win the Flitch Way 100k in 7 hours and 50 minutes, the Spartathlon automatic qualifying time was anything under 8 hours so I would have achieved my goal of qualifying there too had I not got it at the Robin Hood. I didn't know at the time but a 7:50 100k time also meant I'd qualified to run for Wales at the British 100k championships, exciting times ahead. But the road to Spartathlon beckoned, and I was ready to embrace it with all the fire and passion that had carried me this far.

In the weeks leading up to Spartathlon, a meticulous re-evaluation of my training plan took centre stage. The distance – 153 miles –

loomed larger than life, necessitating a recalibration of my approach. A lot of my speedwork was shelved, and my focus shifted decisively towards building a robust aerobic base. Each morning, I embarked on a 2-hour run, followed by an hour in the evening, mostly clocking in at around 8-minute mile pace, with a couple of longer runs of 4 plus hours during the week and one faster session. The steady rhythm, I believed, would acclimatise my body to a sustainable pace over the colossal distance I was aiming for.

My training philosophy was rooted in balance. The opening miles of Spartathlon were strict in terms of cut-offs, so I knew I had to maintain a respectable pace. Yet, I couldn't afford to expend all my energy early on. The key lay in finding a pace that blended comfort and efficiency, recognising that the pace would naturally fade as the race stretched onward. It echoed my approach in the 100-mile race – the strategy was sound, and now it was a matter of executing it on an even grander scale.

A pivotal chapter of my training unfolded under the warm Bulgarian sun during the summer of 2017. For eight weeks, the Bulgarian landscape became my training ground. I got up at 5 a.m., put on my running shoes, and surrendered myself to the road. Each morning's run was a prelude to the day before, I'd get back just as Tori and the children woke up. Later in the day, as the sun dipped, I embarked on a second session, fitting it in between family activities. The training regimen was gruelling but gratifying, churning out about 150 miles a week.

And then came the mountain interludes – days spent in the Pirin mountains, adding layers of uphill and downhill challenges. Ascending some 20,000 feet a week, I felt my strength soar. Those weeks were magical, the culmination of my efforts combined with the breathtaking Bulgarian scenery.

As Greece beckoned and the flight home drew near, there was time for one final litmus test – how would my unconventional training regimen affect my shorter race times? Would I be slower, perhaps even faster? My confidence was building, and as the final countdown to Spartathlon began, I carried with me the echoes of every mile I had run, every challenge I had overcome, The past I had left behind and the belief that I was prepared for the most demanding race of my life.

In the following weeks, I threw myself into a series of races that would serve as both preparation and a gauge of my progress. I set personal bests in the 5k, 10k, and half-marathon, and even claimed the third spot in a county cross-country race. That cross-country podium finish felt particularly sweet, as it wasn't a domain where I initially thought I could excel. The numbers were decent: my 5k now started with a 16, my 10k was at 34 minutes and 32 seconds, and my half-marathon time stood at 1 hour and 17 minutes. These improvements were evidence that my unconventional training strategy was indeed paying off and the countless hours I had spent researching weren't for nothing.

The growing pool of successes instilled a much-needed confidence as the days edged closer to the monumental event. Surprisingly, my nerves remained relatively calm right up until about a week before Spartathlon. I was eager to be at that starting line but still this was unchartered territory and my biggest test to date.

In a span of less than three years, I had traversed a remarkable journey – from labouring through a challenging downhill mile to standing shoulder to shoulder with some of the finest ultra marathon runners in the world. The stage was set for Spartathlon, and I was ready to embrace the gruelling course and the international community of runners who would share this experience.

As the race day loomed, a flurry of doubts began to cloud my mind. Had my training strategy been correct? Should I have sought out more advice rather than relying solely on my own instincts? The questions reverberated – how exactly should I approach this gigantic challenge that lay ahead?

Among the British Spartathlon Team, a strong sense of camaraderie prevailed. In the midst of my internal debates, Darren Strachan, a teammate of mine, stepped forward with a piece of advice: "don't start off too fast!" It might seem like an obvious guideline in a 153-mile race, yet the allure of "banking" some early miles could be tempting, even if it meant potentially running out of steam later on. Darren, meticulous in his preparation, had delved into the splits of previous race winners. His conclusion was that they all began the race conservatively.

The term "conservatively," however, was a relative concept, dependent on each individual runner. Consider the likes of Yiannis Kouros, a true legend of the race. Kouros's pace was so blistering that sceptics initially questioned whether he was cheating, only to later realise that his performances were genuine. He initiated the race with a first marathon time that would have been a personal best for me at the time. But for him, this speed represented control.

Recognising my own capabilities, I knew I wouldn't be matching Kouros's pace. My primary goal was not to secure a top position, but simply to cross the finish line within the allotted time frame. The ultimate reward would be to stand before the statue of King Leonidas at the finish line, a tangible representation of triumph over a challenge that had tested the limits of my physical and mental endurance. In my view, successfully reaching that statue would mark a victory beyond measure.

Chapter 11

Running with Legends

AS I STOOD NEAR THE HISTORIC REMNANTS OF ancient Greece, surrounded by throngs of fellow runners, the reality of the moment began to sink in. Here I was, on the brink of participating in one of the world's most iconic ultramarathons – the Spartathlon. Imposter syndrome started to creep in as the anticipation built. I engaged in conversation with a few of the other athletes, hoping to quell the nervous energy coursing through me. The weight of the impending challenge ahead loomed large, and despite my restlessness, I yearned to begin. Time felt like it stretched endlessly until the starting gun finally shattered the silence.

Amid the initial euphoria, it was a thrill to spot some of the renowned athletes. For months, I had immersed myself in every facet of this race, so seeing the faces I recognised from photographs, articles and books was surreal. I knew that some of these competitors would undoubtedly outpace me, but if I stuck to my planned pace, the cut-off times would be of no concern. There was a mix of excitement and tranquillity within me – I wanted to perform well, yet my primary objective was to savour every moment of this experience.

The sense of reverence quickly gave way as we embarked on this journey, leaving the Acropolis and ancient ruins behind. The roads stretched out before us, and soon the backdrop shifted from historical landmarks to the hum of traffic. I didn't dwell on the enormity of the distance ahead; instead, I focussed on just getting to the next checkpoint. Checkpoint to checkpoint. A horn beep from Tori's car would provide a morale boost whenever she passed, my steadfast one-woman crew.

Although the temptation of the diverse Greek delicacies at the aid stations was strong, I stuck with my own supplies. The checkpoints came and went with surprising swiftness, as the rhythm of running consumed me. Early on, I settled into a pace alongside two other runners. Ian Hammett's diligent training left me convinced he'd be among the frontrunners. Marco Consani, an elite ultrarunner and part of the GB 24-hour team, was a familiar face I had spotted at the race's start. While I was sure he would finish ahead of me, we matched each other stride for stride as we chatted away during the early miles.

Those initial hours breezed by, our steps in sync as if we were gliding on the road. The countless training miles paid off as we maintained our pace without exhausting ourselves. Conversations flowed as the miles unfolded, at a certain point, Marco surged ahead, likely to maintain his elite position. Ian and I continued side by side, a comforting presence during this monumental journey. The weather, favourably cooler than expected, proved to be a stroke of luck. Though still warm, it was far from the searing heat I had envisioned and trained for.

As the kilometres stretched on, the companionship with Ian provided a steady anchor. We shared stories and laughter, cherishing the camaraderie on the long journey ahead. Although there was an immense distance ahead, in this moment, we revelled in the simple joy of running side by side. Approaching the marathon distance our footsteps resonated along the Greek highway, I knew that the true essence of the Spartathlon was unfolding before me.

Seeing Marco's struggle just ahead as we approached the 50-mile checkpoint was a stark reminder of the race's unforgiving nature. The realisation hit hard – anyone, regardless of their capabilities, could succumb to the challenges Spartathlon posed. The race's high rate of DNFs (Did Not Finish) attested to its brutality. As Marco's race came to an end, it was a sombre reminder that this race could easily claim even the most experienced of runners. My heart went out to him as I considered the possibility of it happening to any one of us and for a moment thought about my own hard work and countless hours that would be lost if my own fate had the same as Marco's. I had to snap out of it!

Reaching the 50-mile checkpoint was significant – it marked the transition to more lenient cut-off times. Here, runners could take a brief respite, refuel, and even receive a leg massage if desired. For me, it was a quick replenishment – grab a gel, refill bottles, and continue on. This was one of the checkpoints where my crew, Tori, was allowed to meet me, but as I ran in, she was nowhere in sight. Panic began to creep in, as this was uncharacteristic of her reliability. Had something gone wrong? , She was alone, driving for hours, navigating a foreign country. Despite the racing thoughts, I knew I couldn't let my mind run away with me, I had to stay positive and believe she had just missed a turn or was stuck in traffic. The clock was ticking, and the next checkpoint beckoned just 10 kilometres away, I prayed Tori would be there smiling with a story to tell, grouped with the other crew members.

As Ian fell back, I continued onward, still feeling strong but acutely aware of his absence. The miles didn't fly by as they had with company, but I kept pushing forward. At this point, I was leading among the UK runners, although I didn't let that fact dominate my thoughts. The overall position remained a mystery, but the occasional overtaking of fellow runners fuelled a brief burst of curiosity about how far up the field I might be.

The tension regarding Tori's whereabouts mounted as I approached the next checkpoint. I had mentally rehearsed what I'd do if she wasn't there – a halt, leaving the race, and searching for her if she had been involved in an accident. My mind spun with worry, but as I rounded the bend, there she was – a safe, smiling, and cheering presence. The relief was unmistakeable, and I covered her in a sweaty hug, grateful for her being there despite the earlier confusion. Her getting lost was an amusing mishap, I was to find out later on after the race that she hadn't got lost at all but had been busy taking selfies with the other crew members on the Corinth Canal, she could be forgiven.

With my spirits lifted, I continued on, ready to face the unknown challenges that lay ahead. The ups and downs of the race mirrored my emotional journey, and as I tackled each hurdle, I held tight to the ever-present support of Tori and the camaraderie of fellow runners and their crew.

Pressing forward, my thoughts gravitated towards the extensive training I had undertaken in preparation for this race. The core idea behind my high-volume training was to constantly operate on the brink of fatigue, simulating the conditions I'd face when I reached the 75-mile mark or further. However, this strategy had nearly backfired on multiple occasions, bringing me perilously close to injury. Despite that, I couldn't deny that all those miles I had logged in training provided a significant mental advantage. The prospect of the daunting distance didn't intimidate me; I felt that if I could just keep pushing forward, I would ultimately conquer it.

The miles rolled on ~ 75, 80, 85 – each one bringing me closer to my goal. Surprisingly, I was maintaining a good pace and overtaking fellow runners along the way. At one point, I was informed that I had moved up to the 8th position overall. However, this changed to 9th when Patricia Bereznowska, the women's 24-hour world record holder at the time, gracefully passed me around the 90-mile mark. Still, over 100 kilometres remained in the race, a formidable distance by any standard. While I wasn't yet struggling, Patricia's smooth passage past me did prompt a thought: perhaps I had begun a bit too aggressively.

As night fell, I found myself facing a significant uphill climb. Was this the mountain base, marking the start of the mountain ascent at the 100-mile point? Spartathlon boasts a challenging mountain segment, not a towering peak like Mont Blanc, but a formidable climb nonetheless, especially after having covered 100 miles. Reaching the mountain base, I braced myself for the climb, putting on my jacket in anticipation of the temperature drop at higher altitudes. My friend, Dan Lawson, had previously described this section to me as a "little hill." Coming from someone who had secured second place in Spartathlon and holds the Land's End to John O' Groats record, this description didn't fill me with confidence. However, I remained unfazed, even looking forward to a steep ascent and descent as a break from the constant forward momentum.

The reality quickly set in, and I realised that Dan's notion of a "little hill" was far from my own assessment. Perhaps he had been attempting to boost my morale, though it's more likely that his perspective didn't align with the typical runner's understanding of hills. Dan's standards were a league above most of us, making his characterisation unreliable for the rest of us to measure against.

Navigating the ascent proved challenging, but I managed it without much trouble despite the difficulty. However, upon reaching the peak, I was confronted with a sheer cliff edge drop, guarded only by a flimsy piece of barrier tape. The potential for disaster felt palpable in the dead of night. Despite my fatigue and the haunting darkness, I had to exercise extreme caution; a wrong step could have dire consequences. The subsequent descent was even tougher. The rain had rendered the rocks slippery, and I've never been fond of downhill running, always fearing a fall. I considerably slowed my pace here, especially due to the added effort required to maintain balance on the slick terrain. The darkness likely made the descent seem more technical than it was, although I had anticipated the rocky conditions from my research.

As my pace decreased, so did my core temperature. The chilling wind at the summit of the mountain contributed to the plummeting sensation. I knew that once I reached the bottom, I would regain my momentum and warmth. The descent stretched on for quite a while, and I felt like I was losing valuable time. At this juncture, I contemplated if my brisk start had been an ill-conceived notion or not.

Upon finally descending and finding the aid station, Tori's cheerful and motivating presence dispelled the lingering mountain-related worries in an instant. I enlisted her help in removing my shoes and ridding them of the accumulated gravel from the climb. While she emptied my shoes, I entertained the brief but vivid mental image of my feet swelling uncontrollably, preventing me from putting the shoes back on. I typically wouldn't even consider removing my shoes during a race, but the prospect of running with stones in my shoes for the remainder of the race was far worse.

As Tori helped me wrestle my shoes back on, she handed me a boiled egg and a cheese sandwich from the aid station table. At this point in such a monumental race, these quintessentially British snacks felt like a true indulgence. Unfortunately, my body had other ideas. Despite my craving for nourishment, my system seemed inclined to reject it. I held onto the sandwich and egg for a while, hoping for a change, before discreetly discarding them around the corner. Perhaps one of those scary sounding dogs I'd been hearing constantly for the past few hours could enjoy it.

The mountain descent had shaken my confidence, but even more dishearteningly, I started questioning my role in another runner's decision to quit. During a substantial stretch of the nocturnal section, I found myself running alongside Chad Ricklefs, a prominent American athlete who had previously clinched victory in the fiercely competitive Leadville 100 miler and had represented the USA in the World 100k Championships. On paper, Chad was a much stronger runner than I was, he was a true elite, and I felt a little star struck to be running with such a quality runner, but Spartathlon's unique challenges can render even the most accomplished athletes vulnerable. His previous attempt at the race had resulted in a dropout around the 100-mile mark. As we ran together, fatigue heavy in our limbs, I began to wonder if we might cross the finish line side by side.

However, a moment of mental lapse on my part seemed to cast a shadow over our companionship. During a climb, I posed a simple question, "Are we going up or down?" I genuinely couldn't discern the terrain's gradient at that moment in the dark. His response was marked by a pause, followed by a somewhat dejected, "Oh man, we're definitely going up." Chad's demeanour turned quieter after our exchange, and I couldn't help but speculate on the thoughts racing through his mind. Stranded in the middle of nowhere with a runner who couldn't gauge a hill's slope, he had many miles left to traverse. Shortly after, Chad dropped from the race, leaving me alone to ponder the impact of my peculiar query on his decision.

Guilt gnawed at me as I continued pushing through the night, the realisation that I might have inadvertently negatively influenced someone's race outcome haunting my thoughts. The sense of camaraderie I had shared with fellow runners was slipping away, each of my Spartathlon buddies fading into the backdrop. Marco, Ian, and now Chad, gone one after the other. Despite the melancholic atmosphere, I wasn't prepared to halt my journey. The dawn's arrival promised a renewed sense of purpose, and knowing that Tori was there, driving by and meeting me at checkpoints when possible, lent a flicker of encouragement. My heart ached for my children's absence; being apart from them was always a challenge. Nevertheless, considering the countless training miles I had logged and the progress I had made since that downhill mile back in January 2015, I felt a strong obligation to persevere. Tori had built strong bonds with almost everyone on the journey and was enjoying what she calls "crew camaraderie" with runners and their crews from every country, seeing her happily engaging in the spirit of the Spartathlon also fuelled my determination to get to the finish line.

With a mere 20 miles left, the title of the first UK runner injected a renewed determination into my flagging spirit. Even though a top 10 finish was increasingly out of reach, I held the position as the leading British participant. Occasional reports filtered in about Ian, suggesting he was not far behind me. But, in all honesty, I wasn't concerned with the order of runners around me; I was focused on avoiding prolonged stops to prevent my body from stiffening up.

As the last 13 miles loomed ahead, the promise of a gradual downhill segment provided some hope. I had anticipated picking up speed and allowing gravity to assist me, but my assumptions proved far from reality. The moment I began descending, my quads staged a full-on revolt. The pain was unlike anything I had ever experienced, and a sense of panic gripped me. While I still had a comfortable time buffer, walking the remaining distance had become a realistic yet daunting prospect.

Attempting to ease the soreness, I resorted to a routine of squatting to stretch my protesting muscles, interspersed with brief jogging spurts. It became a mantra of sorts: squat, jog, walk; squat, jog, walk. The agony, a consequence of pushing my body through a half-marathon at the tail end of a staggering 153-mile race. I reminded myself that when I had just started running in 2015, this level of discomfort might have been my experience during the concluding stages of a half-marathon. Now, though, it was an entirely different beast. The fact that I was enduring this ordeal at the conclusion of such an immense distance highlighted the punishing challenge of Spartathlon.

In those agonising moments, I couldn't help but reflect on my preparation – or lack thereof – for the treacherous downhill stretches. If I ever returned to this race, one thing was crystal clear: my training plan needed to include a significant amount of downhill running. It was a hard lesson learned, etched into every painful step I took. If only foresight had been my ally this time around.

An agonising hour dragged by, and I had only managed to cover about 4 miles of the remaining 13. The realisation hit hard – I had hoped to reach the finish within an hour, but at this pace, it was more likely to take 2 hours. My attempts to mix in more jogging between the walks and squats seemed futile. However, I clung to the assurance that if the pain didn't escalate, I would indeed finish. The constant ache persisted throughout the descent, yet somehow, I acclimated to its presence. After all, pain becomes a steadfast companion in the world of ultramarathons; it's a badge of honour we embrace, particularly when the race is over.

Three gruelling hours had elapsed when I sensed that I had finally arrived in Sparta. My memories of the final stretch were hazy, but one image remained clear – the sight of the statue of King Leonidas in the distance. By this point, fatigue had so thoroughly surrounded me that finding the finishing straight was a challenge. A group of young girls from the local running club lent me their assistance, and soon a few kids on bicycles joined them. The finish line was tantalisingly close, and despite my usual emotional reserve during races, I couldn't suppress the surge of sentimentality. I knew that back when I had never even completed a half-marathon, my ambitious declarations of conquering Spartathlon seemed ludicrous to many. Yet, my motivation wasn't about proving sceptics wrong; it was about proving to myself that I could conquer any challenge I set my mind to. It was a lesson I wanted to teach my children – the power of determination and belief.

However, the last thing I wanted was to break into tears in front of spectators. I took a moment to gather myself, determined to maintain my composure for the final push. A mix of emotions – relief, pride, and sheer exhaustion – swirled within me as I readied myself to cross the finish line and carve my name into the Spartathlon history.

I struggled to keep up with the young girls and boys on bikes who had joined me and although I wanted to stop and walk the rest of the way I knew I couldn't, something switched in my mind and at that moment when I thought I couldn't go anymore a rush of fatigued energy spurred me on. As I approached the crowd, I engaged in light conversation with the kids on the bikes, eager to distract myself from the overwhelming rush of emotions. I purposely avoided looking at the statue of King Leonidas, knowing that the sight would unleash a flood of tears. I had visualised this moment countless times, but the reality was more potent than any daydream. Every sacrifice, every arduous training mile, and the weight I shed were culminating in an experience that was simply mind-blowing. Despite the torment my quads had endured over the last few hours, the sight of the finish line injected me with renewed vigour. The body always holds a hidden reserve of energy, ready to be unleashed when the goal is within sight. With a newfound spring in my step, I practically bounded up the steps leading to the iconic statue. Kissing its foot, I paused, taking in the significance of the moment, before turning to face the cheering crowd.

The memories following that achievement remain somewhat hazy. An olive wreath graced my head, and a bowl of water from the nearby river, a symbol of completion, was handed to me, as is the tradition for all Spartathlon finishers. A few girls in white gowns stood at my side and the flicker of cameras blinked before me. I might have taken a sip of the river water, but I was operating on autopilot, attempting to absorb the enormity of what I had accomplished. Then, through the blur of it all, I saw Tori leaping over the barrier and running towards me. It was in her embrace that I finally allowed myself to release the emotions I had tightly held at bay. My head rested on her shoulder, and tears of relief and accomplishment flowed. No one else could see my tears, but Tori knew what this achievement meant to me. She knew the relentless determination, the sacrifices, and the trials that had led me to this point. The pride in her tear-filled eyes was obvious.

Despite the exhaustion, I lingered at the finish line for a while, soaking in the atmosphere.

A blend of euphoria and relief coursed through me. My conviction to finish never wavered. Yet, even before I had the chance to catch a nap, my mind was already contemplating the next challenge. While racing, I am anchored in the present, but once the finish line is crossed, my sights inevitably shift to the next horizon. At that moment, the certainty of returning for another attempt next year filled me, and I was determined to go faster next time.

In 2017, I achieved the distinction of being the first UK finisher, a friendly competition amongst the British Spartathlon Team, a race within the race, and securing the 19th position overall with a completion time of 27 hours, 1 minute, and 41 seconds. Patrycja Bereznowska, who overtook me around the 90-mile mark, would go on to finish in 6th place. Contemplating whether I could have attained her position if I had paced myself differently added a touch of speculation, but I was brimming with joy over my accomplishment. To be among the top 20 finishers in one of the world's most renowned ultramarathons, just under three years after I had begun running, was something that I could forever hold with pride.

Shortly after my feat in Greece, a new aspiration began to form in my mind – to qualify for the Team GB 24-hour team. The concept of this kind of racing intrigued me deeply. In a 24-hour race, there's no predetermined distance; your goal is to cover as much ground as possible within the time frame. Victory is claimed by the individual who best strategises and executes their plan throughout the race. Nonetheless, various factors play into the outcome, and it's highly likely that you'll face significant low points along the way. The challenge in Greece had shown me that I had the potential to cover distances that could position me well in such a race. Most 24-hour events take place on a running track or a looped course, making it a tactical endeavour that's distinct from the point-to-point nature of races like Spartathlon.

Unlike many trail and mountain ultras, a 24-hour race is more of a pure form of running. For years, the world record had been held by Yiannis Kouros, who won that very first Spartathlon. At that point, no one had even come close to his records (although more recently, Lithuanian ultra runner Aleksandr Sorokin broke the

24-hour record with just over 192 miles). However, I wasn't fixated on breaking records; I primarily aimed to qualify for the world championships and represent the Great Britain team. Building up to Spartathlon had demonstrated that this wasn't an impossible feat, but it certainly presented an entirely different level of challenge. The question lingered in my mind – a Team GB vest, could I truly achieve it?

Chapter 12

Racing Adventures and Surprises

IN THE LEAD-UP TO MY NEXT SPARTATHLON endeavour, my journey took me through a series of races, each one another experience. Amid these races, one stood out, not for its grandeur, but for its unadulterated celebration of running – the Barry 40 miler. This low-key event held an allure that was hard to resist, proving that sometimes it's the pure essence of the sport that captivates us most.

Mick, the Race Director orchestrating the Barry 40, understood the essence of ultra running. The event's simplicity was its charm, a 40-mile jaunt around a track – an endeavour that only true running enthusiasts would wholeheartedly embrace. Mick knew this, and he also knew that the delight of the event wouldn't be complete without a quirky requirement – each runner needed a lap-counter, someone to meticulously tally their rounds. It was a race designed for runners by runners, stripped of pomp but bursting with the camaraderie that only those who genuinely love the sport could provide.

As I prepared to join the ranks of the Barry 40, my excitement soared. Conversations with Don Ritchie, the legendary runner who once held the world record for the 100K and 100 Mile distances, had been resoundingly positive about the event and Mick's directorial brilliance. The endorsement of the 100K world record holder was quite an endorsement. But there was more to fuel my enthusiasm – none other than Steve Way, England's representative in the Commonwealth Games Marathon and the holder of the British road 100K record, was also gearing up for the race. I knew I wouldn't be trying for victory against Steve, but that wasn't the point. His transformation from an overweight smoker to an ultra-running sensation had inspired me greatly. He had reached remarkable heights, donning the England vest in the Commonwealth Games, and this race was just a warm-up for his impending feat at the Comrades Marathon in South Africa. Comrades, one of the world's most illustrious ultras, was poised to welcome Steve, and there was noticeable excitement about his performance there.

My motivation for tackling the Barry 40 went beyond the star-studded cast; it was anchored in the event's rich history and the added allure of hosting the Welsh ultra running Championships. Running 40 miles around a track didn't really intimidate me as I knew I couldn't get lost. I chose to fragment it into manageable pieces, visualising 4 one hour-long segments and one final stretch under an hour. The weather was kind, gracing the day with a gentle sun that cast a warm glow without sweltering intensity.

The miles rolled on, and my legs seemed to run in synchrony with my spirit. Steve, hampered by a hamstring issue, had stepped off the track midway, safeguarding his strength for the impending Comrades Marathon. With his departure, I discovered myself comfortably settled in second position. Ahead of me, Alex O'shea, an elite Irish runner, had claimed the lead and held on until the finish, a couple of laps ahead of me. However, as Alex is Irish, I was awarded an unforeseen victory – the status of Welsh Ultra Distance Champion. That gold medal, clutched in my hand, symbolised not just the triumph of the day, but the journey I had embarked upon and I became the Welsh Ultra Distance Champion. I couldn't believe it.

My journey was now filled with moments – from the monumental race of Spartathlon to the intimate ambiance of the Barry 40, each experience chiselled away at my limits while etching memories I would forever treasure. As I looked ahead, the intrigue of the Team GB 24-hour squad beckoned, a realm that promised to push my boundaries in ways I could only imagine.

The Anglo-Celtic Plate 100K which is the British 100k championship, was next on the horizon – an opportunity to don the proud colours of Wales and pit myself against some of the finest ultrarunners in the country. I had been selected after the result at the Flitch Way 100k, I received an email initially from the team manager Arwel Lewis and then confirmation from Welsh Athletics. The prospect was exhilarating, the chance to represent my homeland injecting an extra dose of excitement into my veins. Unfortunately, this time, the familial cheer squad would have to remain at home, for the strategic accommodation choice was to bunk with fellow team members in a caravan. With Tori and the kids back at home, my focus was solely on the impending challenge.

Patrington, near Hull, was the chosen battleground for this ultrarunning skirmish, the course aptly named the Meridian Ultra for its crossing of the famous Meridian line. Joining the lineup of seasoned ultrarunners was a thrilling prospect, and my role as the rookie in the group was met with eager anticipation. The caravan life was a novelty, a communal hub where lessons would be shared, and strategies brewed.

In this team, I was clearly the newcomer, surrounded by seasoned ultra-runners. Their depth of experience was something I eagerly wanted to tap into. When I mentioned running in my old, worn-out Asics that weren't exactly friends with my feet beyond 20 miles, their reactions were mixed with concern and amusement. They kindly, but firmly, pointed out I might be the only one at the starting line without proper footwear. Paul Wathan, one of our team and sponsored by Hoka, was prepping for Italy's challenging Tor des Geants. His insights on gaining sponsorship seemed invaluable, especially if it meant not fretting over the next pair of shoes.

Jeremy Mower and Dan Weston, the other pillars of our team, were both fountains of knowledge. Jeremy had worn the Welsh jersey close to 30 times, and out of those, 15 were for this very 100k distance. Considering his extensive history with the Anglo-Celtic Plate, he was my go-to for strategic insights. Meanwhile, Dan, fresh off his silver medal win from the previous year's race, had his own trove of advice to offer. I didn't get as much time to bond with Gwyn Owen, another team member, since he was lodged with his family elsewhere, but when we eventually met on race day, he came across as genuinely pleasant, it was a good group of lads.

When it came to settling in for the night, I wanted the others to have their choice of sleeping spots. This chivalry landed me on a rather unforgiving sofa. The lack of comfort was balanced by the lively banter and getting to know the team. We all mixed our carbohydrate drinks, with white powder scattered all over the van it was reminiscent of a scene from the TV series Breaking Bad about a couple of drug dealers in an RV, we all laughed as we looked around our tiny caravan, the glamour of international ultra running. As the sun set, my choice to relinquish the comfiest sleeping spot and resign myself to an uncomfortable sofa didn't dampen my spirits. Although, paired with the lengthy six-hour drive from Wales, I wished I'd had a bit more time to recharge. Apart from the shoe situation, which was too late to rectify, I was ready for what tomorrow would bring. I felt right at home with the team. Their warm reception certainly helped ease any pre-race nerves.

The other national teams boasted an impressive array of seasoned runners, some of whom had achieved staggering milestones in their careers. For instance, Jason Cherimann, a prior representative for England in the marathon, was among the top contenders for this race. Tom Evans' reputation was equally formidable. He had recently clinched the 3rd spot in the Marathon des Sables, and would eventually go on to win some of the worlds most renowned races.

Surrounded by these elite athletes, I couldn't help but wonder if I was in over my head.

I admittedly began the race on a swift note, clocking a pace around 6:40. Perhaps the significance of the event got to me, or maybe, deep down, I believed I could finish under 7 hours if everything aligned perfectly. The race format consisted of five 20k loops. I initially kept pace with Dan Weston and Paul Fernandez from the English squad. Their lively chatter filled the air, but I largely remained silent, perhaps still taking in the magnitude of the moment.

As the race progressed, Paul picked up speed and Dan began to drop back, leaving me to tread the course solo – a state I maintained until the finish line. Reflecting on it, having some company around the 40-mile mark might have been beneficial. That's when the consequences of my brisk start became evident, as fatigue set in. With just a bit over 20 miles left, I dug deep, managing to wrap up the race with a respectable time. Being the first Welshman meant that my doubts that I wasn't good enough to be there and fears that the selectors had made a mistake were unfounded.

The day's top honour went to Lee Grantham. Every time he passed me, I'd cheer him on, and in return, he'd do the same for me. There was none of the expected national rivalry. Just pure, unadulterated enjoyment from running alongside such talented individuals. I clocked in at 7:45, landing me in 8th place overall. While I'd hoped to shave off a few more minutes, I was genuinely satisfied with how I performed.

The 100k distance poses its own set of challenges. It's considerably more than a marathon yet doesn't come close to the 100 miles. This makes pacing a bit of an enigma. Many racers usually drop out along the way. Some days just aren't meant to be. One thing that stood out, however, was the camaraderie within our Welsh contingent. We'd celebrate each lap with a high-five and exchange words of encouragement. But as the finish line neared, our high-fives grew weary and our words, reduced to mere grunts. On a side note, I did beat Tom Evans that day, he dropped from the race but technically "in my book" that still means I beat him. Possibly... Well it's probably the only time I'll ever be able to say it, so I'll take it.

As one race finished another was soon on the radar as I'd decided to try a 24 hour race, it was an opportunity to dive into a different realm of racing. It was exciting to have a new goal. The national 24 hour team. Did I have the potential to run for Great Britain? I wanted to find out.

The entire experience at the Anglo-Celtic Plate was uplifting for my confidence. However, life has its way of keeping us grounded, as I soon discovered at the Belfast Energia 24-hour race in July. I had initially hoped to clock around 150 miles. But the day was challenging, the pain was real and I finished at 117 miles. Still, I found value in the experience and made a silent promise to return the following year, aiming to improve.

A more favourable day awaited me at the Essex 50 Miler. I managed to secure a spot just a week before the event, thanks to Lindley, the race director. Without much pre-race strategising, I had the chance to run alongside Craig Holgate for the initial 15 miles. Given his extensive experience, having represented Team GB across multiple distances, I hoped to glean insights about training, nutrition, and the broader world of running. However, as Craig was on the shorter 50k circuit that day, I decided it would be wise not to match his pace for the entirety of my 50-mile journey. Nonetheless, this brisk start gave me a good lead. The course layout allowed me to gauge my position, and I noticed I had created some distance between myself, and 2nd place, Dave Ross.

At the time, I wasn't familiar with Dave, but during our run, Craig had shared a few details about him. He mentioned Dave's remarkable feat of completing over 300 marathons, in addition to a plethora of ultras. Considering this race was just a fortnight after my 24-hour attempt, I wasn't exactly feeling at my peak. However, I dug deep and tried to widen the gap with each out-and-back spur. There was this minor uphill stretch at the end of every segment. Initially, it felt like a mere bump, but after 40 miles, it seemed to take on the stature of a mountain. Even slight inclines can become monumental challenges when you've accumulated miles. I suppose there's a psychological element to it, making some parts of the course feel like, well, a daunting uphill battle.

Following the race, Dave approached me with congratulations on the win. We chatted about our respective races, I was genuinely impressed by his impressive track record. Dave also happens to be a race director. While I haven't participated in one of his events yet, I do intend to in the future.

The summer of races didn't end there, I had the opportunity to join the Dorney Lakes ultra, a timed event, spanning six hours. It serves as a convenient means for many marathon enthusiasts to notch up another marathon towards their goal of reaching the 100 Marathon Club. I headed to the race in the company of two friends from the running club: Paul Harris, the runner I had met on that first night at the club, then gearing up for the Jungle Ultra and Chris 'The Beut' Jones, whose transformative journey through running echoed mine in many ways. The day unfolded pleasantly; I had built up enough of a lead that I could stop at 40 miles with 2nd place unable to catch me in the time left.

As the year came to an end, I ventured into a few winter ultras, each presenting its unique challenges, especially with the chilly weather and potential stretches run in the dark. The muddy trails of The White Rose 60 miler stood in sharp contrast to the Spartathlon I'd tackled merely five weeks earlier. We were initially bound for Tori's parents' place in Anglesey for Bonfire Night. Yet, noticing the race happening on the same day up in Yorkshire, I decided to give it a shot. The plan was simple: drop off the family in Anglesey, head to the race, and then circle back.

I felt dreadful early on but 10 miles in I'd somehow managed to get up to 2nd in the field. The leading runner was nowhere to be seen and so I thought I'd just try and hold onto 2nd place but, being a two-loop course, I noticed at around half way that he was only a couple of minutes ahead of me. He seemed to be moving better than I was and so I figured I'd just try and maintain my own pace, hoping he would slow down later on but he just seemed to get stronger as the race went.

The after-effects of Spartathlon made every incline, no matter how slight, feel like a mountainous challenge. Each step was both a physical and mental test, with Spartathlon's memory lending an extra weight to my strides. My usual upbeat demeanour was replaced by a more determined grit as I navigated the course. Upon finishing, I made a beeline for the sink, a quick clean-up before treating myself to a sugary tea. This was the perfect companion for the journey back, along with the 2nd place trophy in the passenger seat. I loved racing, the previous weekend I had run the challenging Snowdonia marathon in under 3 hours, a great race and one of my favourites.

I barely had time to catch my breath before I was gearing up for the Brecon Beacons Ultra just a week later, a race consisting of two 24-mile loops, winding through the hills with a stretch of canal path marking the end of each segment. There was an added time pressure: I had to complete the course in 8 hours to make it back for my running club's awards evening. This challenge seemed particularly daunting given that the accomplished Tom Evans, whom I referenced earlier and who undoubtedly operates at an elite level, had championed the race the previous year in around 6:30. Finishing would mean immediately hopping into my car for the hour-long drive back.

The weather wasn't exactly on my side, but my legs felt alive as the race began. Energised by a sense of urgency, I surged forward, my pace was brisk but manageable, and, to my surprise, I found myself feeling confident on the downhill stretches. Normally, the fear of a misstep or injury would hold me back, but perhaps the urgency of my tight schedule provided an extra push.

Upon reaching the canal path, a final six-mile stretch lay ahead, with me positioned in 4th place. Feeling remarkably steady, I decided to push a bit harder, taking the risk. The fallback plan was to retain enough time for the evening's awards ceremony, even if I exhausted myself in the process. To my surprise, I progressed into 3rd place. Soon, Charlie Harper, holding the 2nd spot, came into view, just minutes ahead. Alas, the finish line was in view at this point, so catching up wasn't an option. Sam Humphrey clinched the top position, edging out Charlie by a mere minute. Both are exceptional runners. I clocked in at 6:41, a timing I hadn't anticipated. There was a brief window for a quick chat with Sam and Charlie, before hitting the road. After a lightning-fast shower at home, I was out the door once more.

From the soaked moors of Yorkshire to the undulating terrain of the Brecon Beacons, each race added a humble page to my evolving running story. The shared encouragement, the hurdles, and the quiet satisfaction of challenging myself made the journey worthwhile. It served as a gentle reminder that personal growth often lies between small victories and inevitable setbacks.

The culmination of the year arrived with an evening of celebration at the running club's awards ceremony. As I stood there, clutching my Achievement of the Year award for Spartathlon and the top division's top runner award for the second year running, to go along with my 3rd place trophy from the day's race it was a haul I'm not likely to repeat any time soon. It was a fantastic evening to go with a great day.

As the year drew to a close, I took a quiet moment to reflect. I felt grateful for stumbling upon running when I did, and while I was proud of achievements such as representing Wales and completing the Spartathlon, I recognised that there was so much more to learn and achieve in the vast world of running. Admittedly, I tend to quickly set my sights on the next challenge, almost immediately after achieving a goal. This mindset is a double-edged sword. While it's important to pause and appreciate personal achievements, there's a looming fear of becoming complacent, risking the hard-earned progress I'd made so far.

2018 was set to be a year with clear intentions. I aimed for a stronger performance in my second attempt at the Spartathlon come September, drawing from the insights of my 2017 experience. Additionally, I was determined to redeem my earlier performance in the 24-hour race, eyeing a spot in Team GB. While I genuinely felt both objectives were possible, I knew that commitment to training was imperative. More crucially, it was essential to introspect on past missteps in both races and strategise to prevent repeating them. Running, I've come to realise, is a perpetual lesson in growth. As I observed at the Anglo Celtic Plate, even top-tier runners aren't immune to challenging days. There's always room for refinement, new knowledge to acquire, and obstacles to navigate.

Chapter 13:

24 Hours

MY CENTRAL RUNNING ASPIRATIONS FOR 2018 revolved around the concept of time itself. I had my sights set on two distinct achievements, both linked by the relentless ticking of the clock: surpassing my previous performances at the Energia 24 Hour race in Belfast and completing my second Spartathlon within a time frame as close to 24 hours as possible.

The echoes of my initial forays into both races had taught me invaluable lessons. The span of 24 hours is a vast expanse filled with unforeseen complications and challenges. However, equipped with meticulous plans and a resolute mindset, I entered the year with the conviction that I could surmount any obstacle if I executed my strategies.

With the dawn of 2018, I made a conscious choice to narrow my focus. Big changes were on the horizon – Tori and I had committed to homeschooling the kids and embracing more of a nomadic lifestyle. Winters would be dedicated to exploration and travel, while our summers would be spent in the Bulgarian mountains. This decision wasn't a sudden whim; it was the culmination of our desire to break free from the grind that had left us feeling trapped and unfulfilled in the UK. The relentless cycle of work to pay bills had quelled our spirits, and the dissatisfaction with traditional schooling only added to our motivation to change our lives. While commitments like mortgages and car loans might have immobilised others, my past of living abroad without such encumbrances proved to be a blessing, there was nothing stopping us from packing up.

The primary goal in Belfast was qualification for the national 24-hour squad. I used my lessons from the year before to put a plan in place and everything would depend on whether or not the wheels came off. This is always the case, whether aiming for a fast marathon time or a certain 24-hour distance – there are fine margins and the best thing you can do is be realistic based on how your training has gone but still have ambitious goals. Tori was looking forward to going because she enjoys the camaraderie with the other runners' families and joked that it's like a night out for her because it's the only time we are really away from the children. Knowing that she would be happy meant I could totally relax my mind and focus on the task in hand.

The enormity of the challenge was not lost on me. I knew that qualifying for Team GB required the performance of my life. My experience at Spartathlon had provided a glimpse into my capacity to endure beyond 24 hours. While the spotlight wasn't on racing against others, but rather against the clock, I couldn't ignore the incredible talent surrounding me. Elite Irish runners aimed for national records. Standing amongst these remarkable athletes added an exhilarating dimension – a chance to gauge myself against runners of that caliber.

The race commenced on a promising note. I found my stride early, holding onto the pace I had envisioned. In retrospect, my goal that day of covering around 260km might have been overly ambitious. Nonetheless, the initial miles were comfortable, and I found myself leading the race at the 80-mile mark. However, as the race progressed, Eoin Keith and Aidan Hogan surged past me at the 100-mile point. This was entirely okay, but the looming challenge was managing the inevitable low points that would arise.

I was mentally prepared for these troughs and made a solemn commitment: if I had to stop for whatever reason, I would get back out there as fast as I could. Even if my pace was reduced, the key was to keep moving. The minutes lost while standing still would mean precious distance lost in the long run.

Around 15 to 20 hours into the race, the cumulative toll on my body and mind became visible. Every step became a struggle. I battled bouts of nausea and was passed by another runner. My overarching goal was slipping away, and although I hadn't initially aimed for a place on the podium, the fact that I had been in contention for so long drove me to regain my third position. This mirrored the life philosophy that both in running and real life, persistence and patience can carry you through the toughest of times.

Summoning everything I had in me, I pushed through this difficult phase, and with roughly four hours remaining, I seemed to reclaim the vigour I had possessed earlier. Eoin and Aidan had already established a substantial lead, but I was slowly closing the gap. Soon enough, I worked my way back to third position and began lapping other participants. This surge, I believe, was only possible due to my preparation in training. Had I been less rigorous in my preparations, I would have lacked the reserve to surge ahead once my body encountered setbacks. Sharing the podium with Eoin and Aidan was a true honour. Aidan is one of the top ultra runners in Ireland and Eoin's reputation extended worldwide, making it even more rewarding to have finished within touching distance of them.

Ultimately, I covered a distance of 235km, slightly below the then 240km benchmark for Team GB qualification. However, this outcome didn't leave me disheartened. I had run a consistent 24-hour race and was confident that I could improve upon this performance in the future. For context, 235km would have sufficed for Team GB qualification the previous year, I was getting closer.

Energia 24 was not actually my only 24-hour race of the year. I headed over to Norway in November for an indoor 24-hour event. Unfortunately, nothing much went to plan. I was having low point after low point and Tori kept encouraging me to keep going when I got to her but there were changing rooms on the other side of the hall where she couldn't see and so I would sneak in there for a power-nap. At first she seemed bewildered that it had taken me 20 minutes to run round the track but she quickly cottoned on and realised, as I had, that this was not going to be my day. You can't get timed out in a 24 hour race so as long as you can keep moving at any pace it feels worth continuing but perhaps the two big races of the year had taken more out of me than I realised. I couldn't wait to be done running round that gloomy indoor track.I stopped at around 18 hours and 110 miles and Tori and I cuddled up at the side of the track whilst waiting for our hotel check-in to open.

As for Spartathlon, it loomed as a colossal goal, and while I didn't obsess over it as I had before, I meticulously dissected my previous performance. The aim was to uncover areas where I could shave off precious minutes and inch closer to the 24-hour mark. One critical aspect was the extended descent into Sparta, a section that had really challenged me in my prior attempt. My training would consist of rigorous downhill sessions, my quads would take a battering, necessary to make them stronger. Of course, it wasn't all downhill. The race has more flat and uphill overall, and there are only so many downhill tempo sessions and downhill repeats you can do without the quads being trashed completely, so there was plenty of the usual volume too.

Another crucial lesson from my 2017 race was the knowledge that I could complete Spartathlon. The satisfaction of finishing this challenging race gave me the confidence to take calculated risks in 2018. If I pushed too hard and ended up slower or even had to stop, it wouldn't overshadow the accomplishment of having finished before.

Training in the heat of Bulgaria over the summer again helped to replicate the weather conditions I would experience in Greece, or so I thought.

Even with the familiarity of having participated before, the overwhelming atmosphere at the start of Spartathlon persisted. The sensation of standing among fellow runners within the ancient Greek ruins retained its breathtaking allure. Officer Higgins, my dogged pursuer during the Robin Hood 100 miler, had become a friend, shared the start line with me. It was fantastic to be a part of the GB Spartathlon team again, the camaraderie within the team was great.

I started strong, being confident in my training and preparation, knowing that if I could finish in under 24 hours it might just be enough for a podium spot. Some years it would be enough for a win but that wasn't in my thoughts; just to aim for the goal time and see what happened. However, amid this unwavering focus, in the back of my mind I was concerned, worried even.

In the lead-up to the event, an ominous cloud of uncertainty hovered. Rumblings echoed about whether the race would even take place. Unusual weather patterns were brewing – a 'medicane,' a Mediterranean hurricane, was forecast. While stormy weather could be expected during an English autumn ultra, the predicted conditions would be of unprecedented magnitude for Greece, particularly at that time of year.

Despite these premonitions, the race was greenlit. Yet, as I entered the fray, I grappled with another challenge – lingering calf pain that had emerged a few weeks prior. While not excruciating, this persistent ache cast a shadow of doubt. Could my arduous downhill training efforts be nullified? Would my calf withstand the gruelling 153-mile endeavour? I could only speculate.

but as we got going the hints of what was to come weather-wise were present in the drops of rain that kept falling. I have never liked running in the rain and I have to admit my calf was giving me a bit of grief for the first 50 miles or so, but in a way these setbacks helped to further take the pressure off. I adopted a pragmatic mindset: I would persevere until the finish line or until my body conceded defeat, whichever unfolded first.

What struck me during my second Spartathlon experience was the profound role the locals play in enhancing the event. The race serves as a monumental occasion for the people along the route, and their support is nothing short of incredible. Reflecting on both years, I couldn't help but acknowledge that much of the race's charm is attributed to this local engagement. During the previous year, children from the villages would eagerly request autographs, drivers would sound their horns in encouragement, and crowds would gather along the streets, cheering us on with contagious enthusiasm. Without this communal involvement, I mused that certain segments of the race might feel monotonous. As runners, we often find ourselves navigating bustling roads, constantly vigilant of passing vehicles, and sometimes even passing oil refineries. These stretches could be particularly uninspiring.

However, interspersed within these less glamorous sections are breathtaking sights that invigorate the spirit. The imposing grandeur of the Acropolis is truly awe-inspiring, running over the Corinth canal bridge is quite the experience, and the ambiance within the villages – where fig and pomegranate trees dot the landscape against the backdrop of Mediterranean architecture – acts as a delightful counterbalance to the industrial areas. I realised that if the predicted medicane struck, most locals would understandably seek shelter in their homes. Yet, the Spartathlon remains a race where its rich history, combined with the collective aspirations and shared experiences of the runners, creates an unparalleled journey. Recommending the race to those genuinely eager to test their limits seems almost an obligation.

Beyond the 50-mile mark, I managed to deceive my brain into perceiving my calf as fine, thanks to the onset of discomfort elsewhere in my body. This diversion from the calf pain was oddly comforting, allowing me to immerse myself further into the experience, despite the intensifying rain. Though not particularly enjoyable in the moment, the fluctuating rain levels provided intermittent boosts to my mental resolve. When the mountain at 100 miles came I felt good enough to stick to my pre-race plan of trying to get up and over it faster than last time. I was still conscious of the fact that one slip or tumble could end my race but I knew what to expect and so was able to push a little harder.

By this stage, I had worked my way into the top 10, igniting a flicker of hope that my goal might be within reach. However, just a few hours later, my shin decided it had other plans.

"Stress fracture." The words reverberated in my mind, the only logical explanation for the searing agony that gripped my leg. There was no other possibility. My pace decelerated immediately, and soon enough, with 30 miles to go, Al Higgins, whose pursuit had been relentless during the Robin Hood 100 miler, caught up. We ran side by side for a stretch, but the realisation that I was holding him back as we chatted pushed me to let him surge ahead. My reality was now about gritting my teeth and pushing through the pain to secure a finish. I knew there was enough time left for that, at the very least.

The miles dragged on, each step an excruciating reminder of the challenge. And then, with a good few hours left, the menacing presence of the medicane manifested. An absolute nightmare! My heart went out to those runners who still had half a day of torment ahead. The grand run into Sparta, a triumphant final stretch in my previous encounter, turned into a torture chamber this time around. The wind howled mercilessly, rain lashed down in relentless torrents, and my shin throbbed with every stride. The finish line was my singular focus, a sanctuary from this tempestuous onslaught. Yet, even that experience diverged significantly from the previous year.

In 2017, as I triumphantly approached Sparta, the streets had been alive with cheering crowds, local children cycling alongside me, a jubilant escort into the finish. Fast forward to this year, and the heart of Sparta resembled an eerie ghost town in the wake of an apocalypse. The streets lay deserted, bereft of the jubilant spectators who had previously lined its path. Tori, Chris Mills, our dedicated team photographer, Paul Rowlinson, and his lovely wife provided a flicker of support amidst the desolation. As I staggered in, the mayor himself emerged from his rain shelter, offering a brief applause, handing me my trophy and water, and then quickly retreating from the tempestuous scene. 26 hours and 35 minutes, a missed opportunity, perhaps, but I was just so glad to finish.

In the haven of the medical tent, I found Al, huddled beneath a tinfoil blanket, battling the shivers of post-race exhaustion. I congratulated him on his top 10 triumph – a well-deserved accomplishment. I, on the other hand, secured the 13th spot, a placement that still managed to bring me contentment considering the nagging injury. Tori and I had promised to wait for Al, offering him a ride back to the team hotel. As we left the grip of the medicane, my heart swelled with admiration for those who continued to battle the elements and the clock. To complete Spartathlon is a feat, but to defy such brutal weather for hours on end while on your feet? The runners who continued to persevere through those harsh conditions were nothing short of heroic.

Returning to the hotel, a fair distance from Sparta, I had a quick shower before joining Al at the bar. Over a couple of well-deserved beers, we recounted the trials and triumphs of the race. Al radiated joy over his achievement, he would go on to run a stellar race the following year, claiming an impressive 4th place finish but this would be my last Spartathlon for a while, I still haven't been back but a fire inside me promises that day will come.

While my 2018 goals had not all materialised as intended, I found solace in the gritty perseverance that led me to cross the finish line despite the odds. Looking back, it was a year punctuated by achievements – the podium finish at the Energia 24 and a second Spartathlon completion, I also managed to bag a couple of low-key marathon wins and won the Welsh Ultra championship for the second year in a row. The failures often teach more than the successes, and from this year's challenges, I gleaned further insights into the realm of 24-hour racing, knowledge to carry into the approaching year. My ultra-running journey had also forged friendships, and witnessing my friends' remarkable achievements was becoming an integral part of my motivation. I had evolved from a lone runner, with unfamiliar faces all around, to someone immersed in a supportive community of kindred spirits. Yet, amidst all the results, what truly mattered was that running these races brought me joy.

In 2018, I managed to squeeze in some shorter races alongside my longer pursuits. Despite my times hitting a plateau, I felt content with my overall performances. The Barry 40 miler in March saw me finishing 5 minutes slower than the previous year. Still, I secured a victory in the Welsh ultra running championship for the second consecutive year. My participation in the London Marathon was more of a training run, and at the Snowdonia Marathon in October, my time was nearly 20 minutes behind the previous year's although this came just weeks after the Spartathlon. None of this bothered me though. Previously, personal bests had come naturally with weight loss and fitness gains. Now, I was edging closer to the point where specialised training was required for specific distances, while my focus at this time was mainly on building endurance. Pursuing a faster marathon time was less appealing than clinching GB qualification for the 24-hour.

As 2019 emerged on the horizon, I set my sights firmly on this goal. I sought out and spoke to anyone who might hold knowledge I could absorb. My training became specific to running for 24 hours and shorter races were planned purely as training runs to cater to this aspiration. Yet, this year would also usher in a contemplative phase, questioning my running journey as I hadn't since I'd started. Since leaving the UK on a permanent basis more and more of my races required me to travel. Was leaving my family for a few days for my running pursuits a self-cantered act? I missed them so much. Should I be allocating those funds for something more substantial than my personal aspirations? Was I even still enjoying these races? Did I still want to be a runner? These doubts crept in and they would lead me to question my whole approach to life at the time.

Chapter 14:

Kenya

IT WAS LIKE MOVING THROUGH MOLASSES, especially at the start. It seemed counterintuitive. These runners could complete a marathon at my best effort without breaking a sweat, yet here we were, shuffling along at a leisurely 10 minutes per mile. What could possibly be gained from it?

These days, I have a complete understanding of the answer to that question. However, initially, it puzzled me why Kenyan marathon runners would go so slow during their easier runs. Now, I grasp the concept entirely: it's all about optimising their demanding sessions. The logic is simple, even if it wasn't apparent at first. Just because you can maintain a certain pace doesn't mean you should. Speed sessions are designed to stress your body and push beyond your comfort zone. But these sessions are truly effective only if the rest of your runs are at a gentle pace, allowing your body to recover fully. It requires letting go of ego, not caring about what others might think when they scrutinise your training data on platforms like Strava. Running recovery runs at an easy pace that doesn't tax you is the secret. Some Kenyan marathoners, who can complete 26.2 miles in an astonishing 2:05 to 2:08, amble along at 11-minute miles during their recovery runs. These runners are at the pinnacle of the sport, and their remarkable achievements speak for themselves. It's a lesson I've incorporated into the training plans I craft and perhaps the most vital thing I've learned so far when it comes to optimising one's running performance.

But how did I end up in Kenya in the first place? Well, Adharanand Finn's captivating book 'Running with the Kenyans' delved into this very subject, and my motives aligned. Essentially, I yearned to go, observe, and run with the world's best runners to glean insights. Simultaneously, Tori agreed that this would be a profound experience for our children, a chance to witness African life firsthand. And so, that's exactly what we did in November 2018.

Our excitement was barely contained as we flew into Nairobi and spent a night there before catching a small plane to Eldoret, close to the famous Iten, often referred to as the 'Home of Champions.' This is where the majority of elite Kenyan marathon runners train, alongside guest runners from around the globe. Even renowned athletes like Mo Farah have spent months honing their craft there. I had been communicating online with another running coach who was spending the winter in the area. I had sent him money to arrange accommodation and airport transportation for us before our arrival. Tori tends to fret more during our travels, so I wanted to ensure everything was meticulously arranged to put her mind at ease.

The drive from Eldoret to Iten took about an hour, during which I was glued to the window, captivated by the sights of authentic

Africa. I had visited several North African countries before, but none of them quite matched the image I held of the continent. Here, monkeys swung from the trees, barefoot children dashed alongside the road, and the earth was painted in that characteristic dusty blood-orange hue. It was everything I had anticipated, and I couldn't help but watch in awe as it all unfolded. My eagerness to run was palpable, but I had been forewarned about the need to acclimate to the altitude first. Iten stands at an elevation of 2,400 meters above sea level, and if you're not accustomed to such heights, pushing too hard early on can lead to illness.

On our arrival, we took a family walk around the local area. It seemed that everyone's gaze was fixed on us. The stares weren't menacing; they seemed more fuelled by curiosity. Although unsettling at first, we soon discovered that Iten often hosted "Muzungu's," the locals' term for white people – international runners who came to train. However, it was rare for them to bring their families along. With our blonde-haired children and foreign appearance, we stood out. Yet, within days, those curious glances turned into smiles, and we quickly learned how welcoming and hospitable the Kalenjin tribe of the Rift Valley could be. For the initial days, we strolled around, familiarising ourselves with the place and its people. It didn't take long for our children to form friendships and join in daily play with the local kids.

Our time in Kenya profoundly changed our family dynamics. It brought to mind my own childhood, albeit with a significant shift in perspective. My mum had always made the best of what we had when I was growing up. However, compared to life in Iten, we were relatively well-off. People there possessed almost no material possessions. Most of them went without shoes, clad in rags, and their meals were meagre in comparison to what we were accustomed to in the UK. Yet, despite their circumstances, they radiated smiles. There was something about the simplicity of their lives that seemed to make contentment easier to find.

As the days unfolded, I gradually joined the locals on their runs, occasionally opting for solitary outings. The routine was strict and unwavering for Kenyan runners – 6 am and 4 pm were the designated running times, with a potential extra run at 10 am. In the in-between hours, not much else occupied their time except eating, resting, and sleeping. Some runners would squeeze in that extra morning run at 10 am. Observing this lifestyle pattern, it became evident why they are considered the best in the world. The altitude certainly plays a part, but their way of life is equally crucial. Running is their life; there's little room for much else. Witnessing their dedication paints a clear picture, it all made sense.

For a select few, international marathons can secure a financial future for their families. It sounds incredible, yet spending more time with them exposed the broader reality. Amid the likes of Eliud Kipchoge and Emmanuel Mutai, most of the others – considered 'elite' in any other country – pale in comparison to Kenya's true elites. At first, this reality saddened me, but it also sparked an idea. What if some of these runners, who were past their peak in the marathon but still remarkably fast compared to us ordinary runners, could transition to ultra marathons? Could we find sponsors willing to offer prize money for them to attempt seemingly untouchable world records? To an outsider, it appeared logical, but when I initially tried to explain this to them, most just couldn't wrap their heads around it. The concept of running for 5 hours or 50 miles seemed inconceivable, let alone 100 miles or 24 hours. No matter how much

I emphasised that it's a different approach, and they wouldn't be pushing like they would in a marathon, most looked at me as if I were out of my mind. I would have my work cut out trying to make them understand.

I didn't think there would be much I could teach these guys, the fastest runners on the planet. My purpose was to absorb their wisdom. So, I geeked out, sitting by the track for hours after my own sessions, meticulously observing their training methods, running form, recovery techniques – soaking up every nuance to refine my skills as a runner and as a coach. I had sometimes felt like an imposter as a coach, doubting whether my relatively short running experience was enough to help others improve. But I was learning so much in Kenya, I knew I could take this stuff and help others and so my confidence grew as a coach.

The term that incessantly echoed in my mind as I contemplated describing Kenyan running form was 'beautiful.' It genuinely seemed as if running was woven into their DNA; their stride appeared effortless, their motion akin to that of a gazelle. They seemed to glide along, even when maintaining sub-5-minute miles.

Sundays typically marked a rest day, unless they had a race scheduled. Their routines were metronomic: a fasted run at the break of dawn, followed by a chapatti bread and sugary tea that could even challenge the fortitude of the stereotypical British builder. Then, it was feet-up until the second run at 4 pm. In between, they might eat a banana or a bowl of ugali – a type of maize porridge. No fancy diets, no sports drinks, and minimal reliance on technology. Often, I'd join them for breakfast, observing their recovery process. Every insight I gleaned underscored the unfathomable dedication required to reach their extraordinary heights. And even then, only the cream of the crop reaps the financial benefits. It's important to note that their financial motivation isn't driven by greed. Their aim is simply to provide for their families and cover basic living expenses. Many of them adhere to these rigorous and disciplined lifestyles, yet will likely never get the chance to participate in a lucrative race let alone win one.

Meeting Eliud Kipchoge, the fastest marathoner ever, was a great experience. Skye and Summer's interest in the Eldoret Cross Country event led us there, an event open to participants of all ages and skill levels. Eliud Kipchoge was present, not as a participant, but as an onlooker. He engaged with the kids, and shared his plans with us to win the impending London Marathon – a feat he'd go on to achieve. Kipchoge's demeanour radiates warmth and humility. In that fleeting interaction, he proved just as grounded as he appears. He exudes humbleness, yet possesses the rare qualities needed to become the fastest marathoner in history.

The girls enjoyed their races. Skye, not usually as keen on running as Summer, found the idea of racing in Kenya exhilarating. Her crossing the finish line a good lap behind everyone else filled me with pride, she could have stopped at any moment, but she kept on, determined to finish. Summer, the 'runner' of the two, secured a commendable position, landing herself in the top half of the field, among more than 300 participants. Their presence as the only two white kids in the race lent them a touch of novelty with the locals but what an experience for them.

My apprehension about encountering snakes on European trails was amplified in Africa, where a wider array of potentially perilous creatures loomed. Fortunately, I didn't cross paths with any venomous beings. Although we embarked on a safari in the national park, observing zebras, giraffes, and the now-rare white rhino. Monkeys often occupied the trees during my runs, a harmless encounter. During our stay, we lived within a gated compound, monkeys would come and say hello occasionally but for the most part our home was a tranquil oasis amidst the vibrant local community. Despite the quiet exterior, the children always found playmates among the locals.

My time in Kenya was a pivotal learning experience, even if I couldn't wholly emulate the lifestyle there. The Kenyan runners' practice of running at a deliberately slower pace during their easy runs became a significant revelation. I decided to adopt this approach, ensuring that my easy runs didn't challenge me and reserved my full energy for speed sessions. Initially, when I started running, my improvement was driven by the fact that I was transitioning from a slow starting point, but as I progressed, achieving additional pace became more challenging. The concept of running slow to get faster was like a light bulb moment for me.

My dedication to twice-a-day runs or 'doubles' received further validation by witnessing elite Kenyan runners adhering to this routine. Their second run of the day might have been a mere shuffle, but the mileage accumulation was consistent. I've always believed in the value of volume, the less is more approach should apply to the pace of the runs rather than how many miles. Of course the time available to us is a big factor, but a second run of 45 to 60 minutes later in the day can take nothing out of us as long as we drop the pace. Rest is equally important, and with our busy western lifestyles it can be hard to get proper rest when we need it, but there are always small things we can do. Going to bed a little earlier, or taking a short break where you can switch off completely, even reading a book for half an hour rather than trawling the internet can relax the mind more.

Hill training emerged as another crucial takeaway from my Kenyan experience. These runners integrated hills into their regimen, leveraging the terrain for both strength building and engaging different muscle groups. Uphill and downhill running offered distinct benefits – uphill work for core fitness and calves, downhill training for quadriceps strength.

Motivation was the driving force behind Kenyan runners' exceptional performances. Many of them ran as if their lives depended on it, driven by the prospect of financial rewards that could secure their families' futures. While our motivations might differ, we all share the love for running. Whether it's about staying fit, finishing a specific race, or even representing our nation's running team, our individual reasons fuel our passion.

Kenya was teaching me that running is not just a physical endeavour; it's a mindful approach that encompasses pace, consistency, terrain, and, most importantly, personal motivation.

Despite the confusion with what running ultras entailed for the Kenyans I was determined to see what I could do about convincing some of these guys. Having spent some time with them and seen their motivation to succeed and make money to support their families I just knew that if I could help them understand the concept of running ultras some of them could set new standards that would be hard to beat.

Aware that my time in Kenya was limited, I teamed up with a local running coach to lay the groundwork for a running camp for

Kenyan ultra runners. The idea was to bring runners together to train, eat, and live as a team. I would seek sponsorship for their kit and nutrition and arrange for race organisers to cover their expenses for international races, allowing the athletes to keep their winnings.

To gauge interest, I put up posters around town and spread the word among local coaches and athletes. The response was astonishing – over 50 inquiries flooded in within days. Athletes with marathon personal bests of 2:09 for men and 2:25 for women were eager for this opportunity. It was surreal to think that these runners, who could easily win most of the world's marathons, were interested in ultras because they weren't getting the opportunity to race marathons outside of Kenya.

In Kenya, getting the chance to compete abroad often requires involvement with agents or management companies. However, the less mainstream nature of ultras meant that to get these guys out of the country to race they would just need a sponsor, this could be the race organiser, they'd also need a visa, which could be obtained quite easily with an invite to a race.

Explaining the concept of ultras to them, especially 100-mile races, was still proving challenging. No matter how much I tried I just couldn't get the message through that you run 100 miles in one go without stopping to sleep, and you might just have a few quick mouthfuls of ugali at an aid station before carrying on. Nevertheless, a breakthrough occurred during one of my recovery runs when I met John Ewoi, the local coach I would team up with. He shared my excitement for the initiative and mentioned a runner who might be interested. This runner was Arnold Kibbet Kiptaoi, who had represented Kenya and secured second place in the world 50k championships with an impressive time of 2:55. With John's support, I felt confident that this initiative could continue successfully after I left Kenya.

As more interest poured in, I arranged a trial run at the Tambach running track. While initially contemplating a 12-hour trial, I realised that given these runners' incredible pace, a 6-hour trial would provide enough insight. Despite misconceptions circulating on social media about Kenyan runners lacking the mindset for ultras, I was convinced that this trial would prove them wrong. The trial was set for the following Wednesday, a test that I hoped would propel these remarkable athletes into the world of ultra running.

I hadn't held much hope of Arnold turning up to our meeting considering the 8 hours he had to travel to get to Iten, but he arrived on time and was reserved and quiet during our first encounter. Arnold's story was both astonishing and frustrating – despite his impressive performance at the 50k world championships, he hadn't received any further invitations to run ultra races. In countries like the UK or the USA, runners of his caliber would likely have a roadmap for the next few years and a team of supporters. Arnold's immediate agreement to my idea of the Kenyan ultra team was exciting, he was on board and I knew he would stand a better chance than I did of getting the ultra concept across to his team mates as well. Here was someone who had actually been abroad to race an ultramarathon. He did have an invitation to run a marathon in Europe the following month but after that he agreed to come and join our camp in Iten.

However, convincing other runners to take part in a 6-hour trial on a track proved more challenging. Many had never run much longer than 2 hours, and the mental aspect of extended running worried me more than the physical challenge. At the point where it would usually be time to go and eat ugali and relax for the rest of the day, there would still be several hours' running to get through. Would they get to 3 or 4 hours and consider it to be futile? I tried to explain the concept as a 6 hour recovery run, thinking that most of these guys could plod around the track for 6 hours at a pace that would be considered fast for many and still not get too tired.

During one of my own training runs someone called after me,

"Excuse me, coach!" I looked round to see a guy running towards me.

"You are the ultra-running coach, correct?" he smiled, "I want to join your team."

I was a little taken aback, not only that he knew who I was and about my plan, but also that he was so keen to get involved.

"Are you familiar with ultra running?" I asked him, as I did with everyone who expressed an interest.

"Yes, sir. I have run an ultramarathon in London."

I had heard of a Kenyan runner who had been brought over by Adharanand Finn to take part in Centurion Running's Wendover Woods 50 Miler.

"It was a 50 mile ultra race in the woods," he continued, "I was leading at 30 miles but I got cold and my shoes were too tight so I stopped."

This was indeed Francis Bowen, or Bowen to his friends. He hadn't really trained properly for the race and because of the lack of prize money he decided to stop after 3 loops of the 5 when he got cold and was concerned about getting injured.

"Would you have carried on if there had been $2000 prize money?" I asked him.

"Of course Sir, there is no way I would have stopped."

It was an eye-opening moment. Bowen joined the team. With a 2:08 marathon time, his potential for success in ultra races was undeniable. Although speed wasn't the sole factor in ultra running, his performance at the Wendover Woods 50 Miler, where he had plenty left in the tank at the 30-mile mark, indicated that with proper coaching and training, he had the capacity to go on to great things in the ultramarathon world.

Arnold and Bowen's involvement in the team gave me renewed hope that my initiative could bridge the gap between elite Kenyan runners and the world of ultras. It reinforced my belief that the world of ultra running had untapped potential in Kenya.

On the day of the trial, my uncertainty about the turnout grew. Despite having 18 commitments, I was unsure of whether anyone would actually show up. Tori and I left the house around 8am with some supplies in hand, including water, bananas, and glucose. If no one turned up, I figured I could use the 'fuel' for my own training the following week.

As we arrived at the track, a mix of apprehension and hope filled me. Abraham Koech, Amos Kibet, and Silvester Kiplagat were already there. We chatted while waiting, and eventually, Amos Kimutai and

David Cheshire joined us. The planned start time was 9 am, and even though I hoped more would arrive, by 9:05, only five runners were present. I decided to proceed with a short briefing.

While I was slightly disappointed that none of the female runners had turned up, I reminded myself that the fact that anyone had come was fortunate. I laid out the objectives of the trial to the group. The goal was for them to run within themselves, attempting to run an even pace over the full 6 hours. Successful completion of the trial would secure their place on the team alongside Arnold and Francis. They would receive coaching, support for expenses, and eventually train at our camp for international races that I would arrange for them.

I emphasised that they could take short breaks here and there, but any extended pause might lead me to ask if they intended to continue, the clock would also continue to tick. It wasn't until later that I realised just how driven they were to succeed. Many of these individuals would be considered elite marathoners anywhere else in the world, with times under 2:20, but they recognised that here in Kenya such speeds are not enough to compete at the highest level. They needed something else and this could be it.

I watched them prepare for the challenge. It was a testing time for them, both physically and mentally, and a chance for them to prove their mettle beyond the marathon.

At 9:12 am, the trial began. I was filled with excitement, understanding that the next 6 hours would reveal whether these runners were indeed cut out for ultras and if my belief in their potential was justified. The initial laps were completed at around a 7-minute per mile pace – seemingly sluggish for these athletes, yet

I was pleased to see that they were heeding my advice. However, I knew that as the sun rose higher in the sky, the real mental challenge would begin; running in the midday heat was not typical for Kenyan athletes.

An hour into the trial, it was evident that the runners were settling into the rhythm and finding enjoyment in the process. This inspired me to join them for a few laps. As we chatted and laughed while circling the track, the atmosphere was lively. At the 3-hour mark, I changed their direction around the track and handed out bananas. It was at around the 4-hour point that the mood shifted dramatically. David Cheshire was starting to drift back from the main group and I asked him if he was Ok as he passed.

"I'm Ok, just feel like I should slow down a bit so I'm sure of making the full 6 hours."

He certainly didn't look like he was in any kind of trouble but this was uncharted territory, and even these remarkable runners began to exhibit signs of human limits. Abraham felt nauseous and paused for a few minutes, and Amos Kibet started to lag behind the others. The heat, approaching around 40 degrees Celsius, was becoming oppressive.

Conversely, Amos Kimutai and Silvester maintained their initial pace, seemingly unperturbed. They appeared to have plenty of energy left. Tori and I had mixed glucose into the water to create a makeshift sports drink, which we handed to the runners periodically. Amos Kibet downed an entire bottle, seemingly rejuvenated within minutes, almost as if he had used a health potion in a video game. He was right back on pace with the others, almost hovering around the track as if he was just minutes in.

Tori was documenting the event, capturing important details such as David's hard training session the day before the trial – a factor that explained his slight drop in pace. Meanwhile, Abraham revealed he hadn't eaten breakfast that morning. On a nearby hill, curious onlookers, including teachers and students from the local school, observed the unfolding scene, wondering why these men were running laps around a track for hours.

With less than two hours remaining, the challenge was taking its toll, and I thought some might drop out at this point. However, none of them did. Some Kenyan coaches I had spoken to earlier had predicted that a few might give up out of sheer boredom, or that others might run too hard initially and exhaust themselves. While I respected their opinions, I also understood their preconceptions stemmed from a limited understanding of ultra running. I had confidence that the runners, accustomed to slower paces on their recovery runs, could grasp the concept.

In the end, all five of them finished, with Amos Kimutai and Silvester running around 75 kilometres, and the others completing between 65 and 68 kilometres. While this might not sound overly impressive, considering the world 100k record is a bit over 6 hours, it was a fantastic accomplishment for a first attempt, this wasn't a race and it wasn't about speed. They had shown that they could endure for 6 hours, and I felt a mix of relief and emotion witnessing their achievement.

With a solid foundation laid, I was confident that with further training, they could increase their distances substantially. I provided them with enough money to cover their weekly food expenses, urging them to consume a substantial meal to aid their recovery. Yet, I knew they would likely still have a bowl of ugali, despite my advice that they should be consuming a minimum of 3500 calories per day to support their ultra training – a far cry from what they were accustomed to.

Word of the idea spread and it wasn't long before John told me that Dismas Lorita had expressed an interest. Dismas, the winner of the 2018 Mombasa Marathon, was a prominent figure in the Kenyan running scene, known for his rigorous training in the Nandi hills, where he regularly covered 70k distances. I met with Dismas at the Elgon Valley Hotel, he had brought his friend, a lady called Ziporah Eleman. Ziporah had recently won a marathon in Peru but had a strong desire to transition from road marathons to trail ultras. She quickly grasped the distinct training approach required for ultras compared to marathons and agreed to join the team. I looked forward to working with her. The inclusion of a female athlete was particularly exciting, as longer distances often level the playing field between men and women.

Dismas shared that he completed 70k runs in just over 4 hours—an impressive feat, especially considering the lack of fuel, challenging terrain, and an altitude of almost 8000ft. I believed that with proper training and the right mindset, he could potentially break the 100k world record in the future.

As March arrived, the team was settling into their ultra training, focused on increasing their volume while still including a weekly speed session. Through Adharanand Finn's connection, I was put in touch with Ed Smith, the race director of the Belfast Energia 24-hour race, who expressed interest in having a Kenyan runner participate. Having met Ed previously in Belfast, we devised a plan to bring Amos Kimutai to the event. Amos had recently taken part in the Kilimanjaro Half Marathon in Tanzania with no specific preparation for the distance and had managed to finish on the podium against strong competition, he'd also won a local marathon. His performances indicated he was in decent shape.

As our time in Kenya came to an end I was confident in leaving the team in the very capable hands of coach John Ewoi. Upon returning to Europe I arranged meetings with potential sponsors for the team. While many companies expressed interest, securing commitments was challenging. Understandably, sponsors wanted to witness the Kenyan runners' performance before offering support, a catch 22 situation making it difficult to get the athletes to showcase their potential.

The ultra-running community demonstrated immense generosity, as I requested kit donations at the race Tori and I were organising in the UK (The St Illtyd's Ultra.) I was overwhelmed by the assortment of gear, including bags, tops, shorts, and more. Rupert Coles offered a Garmin watch, and my friend David Bone donated a box of running shoes. These acts of kindness significantly aided individuals who couldn't afford such equipment and highlighted the strong sense of unity within the ultrarunning community.

However, my efforts to introduce elite Kenyan runners to ultra-running encountered resistance from certain quarters. Some believed that including these athletes would undermine the essence of the sport. A portion of the community clung to the notion that ultra-running should remain niche and free of elite runners. To me, the beauty of ultra-running lies in its inclusivity – with fast runners vying for victory at the front and those farther back striving to finish. Unfortunately, there were those who feared that Kenyan runners might sweep prize money and vanish back to Africa. I

Puddings to Podiums | 155

found this perspective disappointing, as I believed that helping these talented individuals improve their families' lives could only be a positive endeavour.

While this viewpoint was held by only a minority, it saddened me to see such reluctance. I held onto the hope that over time, some of these Kenyan athletes would make a significant impact on the world of ultras, much like East African runners transformed the marathon scene in previous years. I firmly believe that everyone should be welcome to participate in these events. I remained committed to doing my part to make that happen. The addition of Kenyans on the start lines would inevitably mean that I wouldn't win as many races as I had done, the only downside!

Our time spent in Kenya left an indelible impact on our family, reshaping our perspectives and making us better individuals. It was a powerful reminder that true happiness isn't necessarily tied to material possessions. We interacted with people who owned very little but radiated joy, a lesson that deeply influenced all of us. I hope this lesson remains ingrained in my children's hearts as they begin to navigate their own paths in life. While I wholeheartedly support any aspirations they may have to earn well, possess nice things, and achieve their goals, I also want them to recognise that genuine happiness can be found without these external markers. Experiencing life in Iten illuminated this profound truth – that the abundance of "stuff" isn't a prerequisite for happiness.

Amos Kimutai never did race in Belfast, I do remain optimistic about the future though. I look forward to witnessing these remarkable individuals, whom I'm fortunate to have worked with, triumph in ultra-distance races around the world.

Chapter 15

DNF (Did Not Finish)

"CAN'T YOU JUST COME WITH US, DADDY?"

Jackson's innocent question echoed in my mind as I navigated the boiling Tennessee roads. While I was running in solitude, Tori and the kids were exploring America in the comfort of an air-conditioned car. This race had been an incredible experience, but the feeling of guilt began to creep in, especially when Jackson's plea reminded me of what I was missing out on.

Before heading to the States there were some races back in the UK I had gone back for. The excitement I once felt seemed to be fading. Starting with the Barry 40 in March. That race held a special place in my heart, but in 2019, things were different. Armed with lessons learned from the intense winter training in Kenya, and the gains made from training at altitude, I had hoped to translate that into a strong track performance and finish in around 4 hours. This would have allowed me to retain my Welsh Championship Medal for the third year in a row. However, my race didn't go as planned, and I found myself absurdly contemplating quitting with just 3 miles left. This wasn't due to injury or dangerous weather conditions, but rather because I wasn't having a good race and wasn't in contention for the win. I grinded it out for the final few miles, finishing in 3rd position, but I hadn't enjoyed myself at all. Looking back, I feel a sense of embarrassment that I almost let my ego overshadow the joy that running had always given me.

I was beginning to realise that I was shifting my priorities for these races. While aiming for ambitious goals was important to justify the expenses and time away from my family, I was losing sight of the core essence of running. Nearly giving up on the race just because victory wasn't within reach was contrary to the spirit of the sport. The thrill of finishing a race, regardless of the outcome, was what had initially drawn me to running. Reflecting on that moment, I tried to realign my mindset and remember why I started running in the first place.

Next up was the Anglo Celtic Plate UK 100k championships in Scotland, where I would be representing Wales once again. Despite the honour of running for my country, as I arrived on that chilly day and felt the icy air pierce through me, thinking of Tori and the kids back home in Bulgaria, I couldn't help but question my decision to be here. Racing in freezing temperatures had never been my preference; the biting cold numbed my body and dampened my spirits. While warming up comes naturally as you get moving, slowing down even slightly exposed me to the brutal cold, making the experience rather unpleasant.

With a goal time of 7:15 in mind, I was determined to push myself. However, things didn't go as planned. The frigid air took a toll, and I had to contend with a couple of moments of sickness. For a meticulously calculated goal like mine, any deviation meant losing precious minutes, which put me in an uphill battle.

As the miles ticked away, the negativity in my mind grew louder. Doubts started to swarm, and I felt an urge to stop. In that moment, I began to resonate with those who questioned the sanity of ultra-running. The thought of a cozy environment, maybe sipping on a pint of Guinness in front of the fire back at the team hotel, seemed much more appealing than pushing my body through this ordeal.

And then I made a decision. At the 46-mile mark, I decided to call it quits. With only 16 miles remaining, I reasoned that it wasn't worth pushing forward when my initial goal seemed unattainable. Holding that pint of Guinness back at the hotel felt like a warmer and more comforting option. I wasn't injured, I was running for my country, I should have finished.

Runners like Charlie Harper who finished in an impressive 6:40 on that day was in a different league to me. Was I really good enough to be trying to compete at this level? Had I been winging it the past few years? What on earth made me think I could qualify for the national 24 hour team? I couldn't even finish a 100k. Others would tell me that this self-doubt was misplaced, but they were just trying to make me feel better about myself. I guess part of my running journey was about pushing myself as far as I could go. When it felt like I was reaching the limit there was a sense of deflation; where could I go from here?

Despite almost quitting my first 50 miler, finishing that race had paved the way for some of my best racing experiences. However, those times felt distant now, and my passion for running was waning.

My family's importance trumped everything. Although I had always known I would reunite with them after races, the new reality of travelling alone to the UK magnified their absence. I hated being away from them.

The Grand Union Canal Race (GUCR) of 2019 was my goal race for the first part of the year. While it couldn't exactly match Spartathlon's grandeur, this 145-mile event every May held a place in the UK's major ultra races. Stretching from Birmingham to London along the canal, it promised a flatter route and more forgiving temperatures compared to Spartathlon. My aim was clear – run under 24 hours. I hadn't been quitting races because my training had been going badly; I just believed that not meeting my goal justified preserving myself for the next challenge. At least that's what I was telling myself. The fact is I just didn't have the same hunger as I'd had before, I'd stopped caring. I needed to find my 'Why' again, get that hunger back, and this was my chance.

Carrying Dan Lawson's course record in my thoughts, I stood at the starting line of GUCR. A sense of uncertainty. As the race kicked off from Gas Street in Birmingham, I focused solely on the task at hand – finishing. Get it finished and I can get on that flight back to Bulgaria and back to my family. The unease of leaving them was definitely impacting my performances that year.

The race started well. I raced ahead, on course record pace, feeling at ease. But what's comfortable at mile 30 isn't the same at mile 60. A sub-24-hour finish was my goal, and for the initial 60 miles, I was ahead of schedule. This time, my training aligned, and race day felt smooth. I progressed steadily, conscious of not overexerting myself. The flat canal path had its own challenges, straining muscles in a distinct way from hilly terrain. However, things started to fall apart just before the 100k mark.

I hit the most formidable wall you could imagine. I think I was leading by about 4 miles before I had to start walking. My stomach revolted, dizziness set in, and I scrambled for a discreet spot to puke. I hoped for instant relief, but it didn't come. I aimed to walk for a few minutes and recover – a plan that quickly unravelled. What followed was a disheartening trudge. With mates Darren Strachan and David Bone (Daz n Bone) kindly traveling down to support me, I was undoubtedly a sombre presence. Yet, as fellow ultra-runners, they understood my struggle. They kept Tori informed over the phone, she'd also try to motivate and encourage me.

I would learn later on that David had actually really gone above and beyond to be there for me. A month before the race he'd been bitten by an insect whilst on holiday in Sri Lanka, he'd been to the hospital several times after the bite had gotten infected. He wasn't feeling great, He didn't tell me until much later but he actually passed out when waiting for me at one of the aid stations!

The support they offered was remarkable, they later told me that they were convinced I would win and had even planned to look after the winner's trophy for me as I wouldn't be able to take it back to Bulgaria on the plane. But when they arrived at Mile 63, I was already struggling. Their plans to celebrate a win were met with my diminishing hope. I was struggling to find the drive to continue.

After a few miles of walking, Alex Whearity, the eventual winner, passed by me and stopped to see if I was ok. "Feeling sick for ages, mate," I groaned. In response, he handed me an Imodium tablet, and though grateful, I encouraged him to keep moving. I knew he'd be glad to see me walking, he was a competitor too, but his act of kindness touched me. The ultra-running community is marked by such kindness.

Time slipped by, and while no one else overtook me during the 20 or so miles we had been walking, Darren and David assured me I was still in the race. But motivation to catch up with Alex or stay ahead of 3rd place had deserted me. I had lost all interest. Somewhere around the 90 mile mark, I threw in the towel, again.

The guys gave me a lift into London, I booked a hotel for the night whilst lay in the back of David's car, and soon I found myself at the hotel bar. I reflected as I propped up the bar until close. The support from David and Darren that day deserved more from me. After a few hours sleep, I made my way to the finish line to cheer in the finishers, an experience I enjoy. Oddly, I had no regrets the following morning about not finishing myself, even though I knew it was possible within the cut-off time. Losing the race win had sapped my motivation, a decision that still bothers me. Why didn't I just keep going? My support crew of David and Darren had gone above and beyond, and I should have persevered for their sake, even if not for my own.

Watching others accomplish their goals was fantastic, yet my love for racing was waning. It had transformed from pure enjoyment to a strenuous effort. As I mentioned earlier, being away from my family played a significant role. My sole success so far that year came during the Crawley 12-hour race, where Tori and the children were with me in the UK. The win though was a result of others' struggles as much as my own perseverance.

I had started taking my coaching career more seriously after my first Spartathlon. Despite initial hesitations due to my relatively short running career, I hoped to demonstrate the effectiveness of my training methods. I was working with athletes from all over the world. My approach combines exercise science and physiology, training theory, and the crucial task of instilling belief in the athletes. Looking back at my own running career, what I believed I could achieve might have seemed far-fetched to most, but setting big goals, visualising them, studying the science, and putting in the effort is how we achieve the seemingly impossible. Ultimately though I want my athletes to enjoy their running and I always try to remind them that it's meant to be fun. This is what I lost sight of in 2019 and so the races I entered were largely unenjoyable.

The main draw of coaching, for me, was the opportunity to help others derive the same fulfilment from running that I had. Over a few years, I absorbed nearly a decade's worth of training theory, which aided in establishing myself in this field. My own training obsession had driven me to continually seek improvements, and I wanted to share that drive with others.

This not only allowed me to support others but also provided a channel for my shifting goals.

As I had watched runners who were on another level to me, doubts crept in. The gap appeared insurmountable, making me question the purpose of my own racing. It was clear that the work I was doing instilling self-belief and motivation in my clients needed to be directed inward too. It was time to get stuck into my own mind again!

Team GB qualification was where it was at. That's all that mattered. The World 24-hour Championships in France awaited me in September, with that qualification goal firmly in sight. I believed that by applying the lessons learned and new perspectives, I could meet the qualifying standard. If I achieved it, it would signify new horizons. If I fell short, uncertainty loomed. Experiences in life were shifting the importance away from racing but underneath it all was still a burning ambition to get the very best out of myself while I was still young enough to be able to reach the pinnacle of the sport, running for Great Britain.

Chapter 16:

Vol State

IN THE JUNE OF 2019, WE DECIDED TO HEAD TO
America for a holiday, or at least that's how I sold it to Tori, naturally,
I couldn't venture all that way without entering a race. The Vol State
500k had been on my radar for a while, it's the brainchild of the
legendary Lazarus Lake, the same mastermind behind the Barkley
Marathons and the concept of the Backyard Ultra. Laz's races are all
about pushing the boundaries of human endurance and attracting a
unique breed of runner, though each race stands distinct. Take the
Barkley Marathons, for instance – an utterly insane race comprising
five loops spanning 20 to 27 miles (depending on who you ask)
in Tennessee's Frozen Head State Park. It boasts a jaw-dropping
elevation on each loop, exceedingly technical terrain, erratic weather
conditions, virtually no aid stations (except one with water midway
through the loop), and the challenge of locating between 9 and 14
books dispersed around the course and collecting the pages that
correspond to your race number, a different one for every loop;
if you fail to present all your collected pages at the start/finish,

you're disqualified. A mere 15 individuals have ever completed the race in its entire history, illustrating its nearly insurmountable difficulty. The course record hovers around 52 hours, underscoring its monumental challenge.

In recent years, the Backyard Ultra concept has gained worldwide recognition, but Laz started it with a race where participants tackled a 4.167-mile loop of his garden within an hour. This cycle repeats, and runners re-commence the loop each subsequent hour until only a single participant remains. This race has witnessed some truly remarkable feats in recent times.

Vol State, however, stands apart. It's a point-to-point race stretching through Tennessee, briefly cutting through Missouri and Kentucky at the start. Throughout the entire race, you're responsible for yourself, although you can decide whether to be "crewed" or "screwed." If you're crewed, a support crew in a vehicle can supply you with drinks along the way. You're permitted to enter the car when it's stationary, but if it moves with you inside, you're immediately out of the race. If you choose to be uncrewed, or "screwed," you're fully self-reliant. Yet, over the years, the race has gained popularity in the local area, leading to the emergence of "road angels" – people who leave coolers by the roadside stocked with supplies for Vol State runners.

I have a feeling Laz might have mixed feelings about this development. While he's undeniably compassionate and genuinely cares for participants, he possesses a wicked sense of humour. If he senses his races are becoming "easy," he's known to introduce further challenges to heighten their difficulty. This is especially evident with the Barkley Marathons. Whenever someone manages to complete the race, he adds an even more monumental hill to the course the following year. In recent times, only a handful of people have finished the race.

Vol State presents its own set of challenges. The relentless 100% humidity turns running into a gruelling task during the daylight hours. Adding to the complexity, local individuals with questionable intentions, often referred to as "rednecks," might try to intimidate runners. Unfortunately, there have been instances of harm, with a competitor recently being hit by a car. Rattlesnakes, aggressive dogs, and, of course, the sheer distance itself contribute to the test. Typically, the winner covers the course in around three days, while some take as long as ten days. As for me, I had no definite plan – whether I would vie for victory or merely focus on finishing. Yet, Laz's portrayal of the race on the official website convinced me that attempting it was an absolute must " The Vol-State is not just another ultramarathon. It is much more than that. The Vol-State is a journey, an adventure, and an exploration of inner space. It begins with a ferry ride across the Mississippi River, from Missouri to Kentucky, and finishes at "the Rock," high atop Sand Mountain in Northeast Georgia. What lies in between are 314 miles of the great unknown. From the time the Vol-Stater steps off the Ferry, until they reach the Rock, they are totally reliant upon their own physical and mental resources. For the next three to ten days, in the face of the heat and humidity of July in Tennessee , the Vol-Stater must make their way on foot, along highways and backroads, from one small town to the next, over hills and across rivers, up mountains and down long valleys, all the while accounting for all of their most basic needs; "what will I eat?" "When will I find water?" Where will I sleep?" Success is not guaranteed. There are no aid stations, teeming with volunteers waiting to tend to your every need and encourage you to continue. There are just miles and miles of empty road. Your friends can follow your progress from afar, but no pacers can carry your burden for you. If you do encounter another runner, theirs is the same desperate plight as your own. You will have doubts. Finishing will often seem an unfathomable dream. Your worst enemy may become the knowledge that an air-conditioned ride to your car at the finish (in the dreaded seat of disgrace) is but a phone call away. Many will fail. But, for those who find the steely will and muster the sheer dogged tenacity to overcome the impossible obstacles, and reach the rock on foot, the Vol-State can be a transcendental experience. No words can adequately describe the sense of combined relief and amazement to be experienced at the Rock. No one can explain the regret that this incredible journey has actually come to an end." one past competitor noted, "During this race, I found something in me I never knew was there."

This sentiment is a familiar refrain among many who undertake ultramarathons, but there's something uniquely profound about Vol State's self-sufficiency aspect and the previously mentioned challenges that's bound to leave its mark on anyone taking part.

The race begins with a brief jog onto a ferry that crosses the Mississippi River, transporting racers from Missouri into Kentucky. After that, it's all about putting one foot in front of the other. With so many miles stretching ahead, calculating a sensible pace becomes nearly impossible; it's more about relentlessly moving forward, eating when hunger strikes, drinking when thirst beckons, and resting when fatigue overwhelms. If your aim is to win, sleep might be something to minimise, but surprisingly, a quick power nap can sometimes perform wonders during a multi-day race. You can be teetering on the edge of a mental breakdown, and then a brief snooze can rejuvenate you, transforming your state of mind.

For this race, Tori was going to be my support crew. However, this time, she would be with by the kids, which meant she wouldn't be able to meet me as often as usual. In fact, once the race commenced, I didn't see them for quite a few hours. They found their way to a swimming spot while I continued my journey, we would meet up later in the day. Laz insightfully points out in the race description how sometimes having a crew can be somewhat of a disadvantage. When the going gets tough, the allure of an air-conditioned car and the presence of your loved ones can make it exceedingly hard to resist the temptation to quit.

In the lead-up to the race, our journey was marked by unexpected challenges. Storms in New York led to the cancellation of all connecting flights, leaving us stranded there for two days that hadn't been factored into our plans. Surprisingly, this turned out to be a blessing in disguise. The unexpected delay allowed us to embrace the tourist experience. The kids were thrilled to see the Statue of Liberty, and we enjoyed some quality time exploring Central Park – the perfect introduction to the United States.

On a personal note, I was fortunate that our time in New York coincided with the Sri Chinmoy Self-Transcendence 3100 race. This event is a 3,100-mile undertaking, involving repetitively completing a small loop of a city block in Queens. Runners take around 50 to 60 days to finish it. While very few participants attempt the race, I was eager to join a few of the runners for a lap each, as allowed by the race rules.

We took a taxi to Queens, and I had the opportunity to watch a segment of this unique "race." Todor Dimitrov, a Bulgarian runner, was taking part and we have some mutual friends back home so I ran a lap with him and we chatted a little bit about our common ground. I loved the experience and wished him all the best after a short time when the lap was complete. I then had the privilege of running with Ashprihanal Aalto, a legendary figure in this niche of ultra-running. He holds the course record of 40 days for the race and has won the race around 10 times. It's a form of ultra-running that remains quite exclusive due to the significant time commitment required for a 40-50 day race each year.

After leaving New York and arriving in Tennessee, we rented a car and embarked on a journey, eventually arriving in Union City, Tennessee just in time for Vol State. Along the way, we visited iconic places like Graceland in Memphis and enjoyed ourselves in the child-friendly country and western bars in Nashville.

The beginning of the race, true to Lazarus Lake's unique style, was marked by him lighting a cigarette..

In the early stages I was running well within myself but still somehow found myself well in front of the other runners. Of course, if I look back now I can see that the others runners knew something I didn't, but at the time it just seemed like my race was going extremely well. Perhaps I was grappling with a bout of over-ambition that year, for on more than one occasion, I managed to build a substantial lead over my closest competitor in the early stages of races. A decision that would prove less than wise, as it had before. However, in the moment, I revelled in the belief that everything was falling perfectly into place. Yet, the frequent site of armadillo carcasses strewn by the roadside did dampen my sprits slightly. In the UK, it might have been foxes, badgers, or deer, but encountering such a grim site of these unfortunate creatures made me sad.

My spirits were soon lifted by the site of a roadside cooler box with 'For vol state runners' written on the side in marker pen. An act of kindness by the legendary road angels. When I peered inside, I was absolutely delighted to see freshly cut slices of watermelon. Taking one and sucking the moisture from it along the way was a massive boost in such extreme humidity. Staying hydrated is hard at the best of times but in these conditions it was pretty much impossible. All you could do was damage limitation, and I've found watermelon to be one of the best ways of doing this. I'll often have a pack or two of watermelon slices for 24 hour races to give me a break from the gels.

Laz and his team made sporadic rounds to check on runners, but given the immense 300-mile course, these encounters were rare. Thus, we were required to phone his mobile twice a day, at 6 AM and 6 PM, just to let him know that we were still alive out there. Various strategies were employed by runners - some take a break during the hottest part of the day and then keep running into the night, some get as far as they can in daylight and sleep during darkness. There was no formula, no right way. It was a personal journey. My approach wasn't meticulously structured, but I was eagerly embracing this unique experience that had built up considerable excitement. The beginning of the journey was living up to my expectations. The state of Tennessee was not disappointing me.

Tori didn't have times to stick to as to where we would meet so it was always a nice surprise when I saw her and the children. I ran for 8 hours alone to begin with and would occasionally pass a shop or a gas station. With those and what was left by the road angels I was never short of supplies. As I journeyed, I relished the diverse sights, occasionally passing through small towns where families cheered me on, reminiscent of Spartathlon.

Further down the route, I was informed about the unexpected comforts awaiting. Pop-up tents and hammocks were available for runners to rest. Having existed for over two decades, the race had woven itself into the local culture, offering a source of anticipation for the communities. While not everyone exuded warmth, the majority of individuals were incredibly welcoming. Their generosity and assistance left an indelible mark on me, making me aspire to adopt more of these qualities in my own life. In one town, I stumbled upon a Farmers' Market stall adorned with a sign that read "Vol State runners this way." Following the indication, I was greeted by an exuberant stallholder showcasing a variety of treats. As I reached for some dollars, he simply said, "No, no. Take what you need!"

This gesture of kindness left me utterly amazed, a sentiment that would repeat itself over and over throughout the journey. Cooler boxes brimming with water, beer, ice creams, and more appeared along the way. Fire stations and churches transformed into makeshift aid stations, offering ice pops, beverages, and even soothing leg massages. This hospitality and generosity were not part of the race itself just acts of kindness selflessly undertaken by these institutions.

The lead changed a few times early on between me, Johann Steene and Greg Armstrong. Johann is a legend of Laz's races, having previously won the Backyard Ultra and been brave enough to take on The Barkley Marathons. Greg was a previous winner of this race, and I was amazed to see he would be running the whole race in sandals.

His devout Christianity was evident in his charitable, kind, and humble nature, all coupled with impressive running capabilities. By the eighth hour, Johann and Greg were conspicuously absent behind me. This should have been a telling sign that my performance might replicate that of the GUCR – too fast a start would leave the ending almost inevitable.

Around the twelfth hour, the relentless heat finally caught up with me. What had previously been a comfortable pace now felt hard to maintain, eventually leaving me in a state of utter exhaustion. The collapse was as remarkable as it had been at the canal race. One moment I was moving with ease, the next I was walking and struggling to stay upright. It was hard to imagine I would feel any better any time soon. My pace slowed drastically, with walking replacing running. As the night descended, I reached a town where it appeared every resident owned a ferocious guard dog, none of them leashed. The eerie glow of my headlamp illuminated sets of menacing eyes, soon accompanied by fierce barks that pierced the silence of the night, sending shivers down my spine. While I had been forewarned about this, the actual experience left me genuinely frightened. Equally terrifying were the sporadic encounters with groups of rowdy rednecks in pickup trucks. They would speed past me, taunting me with unfriendly jeers of "Get off the road," beer cans in hand. The distant roar of their engines would herald their approach, followed by the sound of their voices. It dawned on me just how isolated I was out there. It wasn't exactly the moment to feel as though I could barely muster a run.

Around the 90-mile mark, Tori and I met. I was already struggling, and with a motel nearby, the decision was easy – it was time for a rest. Laz's warning about comfort being the ultimate adversary became glaringly clear as soon as the refreshing water from the shower touched my skin. I could have spent hours under that shower's invigorating stream. The bliss of having the road's dust and stinging sweat rinsed away. The relentless heat had caused severe chafing, so it was also a huge relief just to stop moving for a while. Lying on the bed soaking wet straight from the shower, my plan to resume running in a few minutes was nothing more than a self-deception. The gentle hum of the air conditioning lulled me into sleep within moments. The soft sheets cradled me, providing an unexpected oasis of comfort amid the gruelling race.

I woke up several hours later, my body feeling slightly rejuvenated, but the idea of venturing back onto the arduous road felt ludicrous when my family was right there, offering a haven of safety and comfort. Yet, I reminded myself that I hadn't come all this way to surrender to fatigue. I wasn't injured, just tired, and I owed it to myself to get back out there. But as I rose to my feet, a violent wave of nausea surged over me, forcing me to rush to the bathroom. The turmoil within me was accompanied by dizziness, a disorienting sensation that eventually went away after a few minutes sat at the edge of the bed. Gathering myself, I stepped out and, not wanting to disturb my family, managed to slip away to a nearby gas station. There, I found solace in a bag of salty crisps that promised to be a companion on my ongoing journey.

I tried to get myself jogging, hoping that my legs would loosen up and I could actually break into a run, but it quickly became obvious that wasn't happening. I just walked and walked. The chafing, as though a cruel companion, tormented me mercilessly. The raw skin was a painful reminder of the race's brutality. My shorts, once black, now bore the imprint of the race, transformed to an almost ghostly white by the salt in my sweat. Every time my shorts rubbed on my skin the salt got into my bleeding sores and the pain was almost unbearable. I found myself teetering on the brink of surrender. The idea of enduring hundreds of more miles like this appeared almost absurd. But I resolved to keep moving, if only to reach the next rendezvous with Tori and my children. I would reevaluate from there.

By the time Tori and the kids had woken up, had breakfast, and caught up with me, I had been trudging along at a snail's pace for around 5 hours. Asking them to meet me a bit farther down the road. Half an hour later, I reunited with them, the intervals between our meetings got shorter each time. Stepping into the car brought sweet relief, but each time the icy grip of the air conditioning seemed reluctant to release me from its embrace.

As I moved ahead with a combination of feeble jogging and determined walking, I could almost envision Laz, the mastermind behind this race, rubbing his hands with glee, knowing the test that lay before me. The scene played out with Tori, now driving just a few hundred meters ahead, and I slowly trudging to catch up. In her gentle way, she attempted to coax me into continuing, but it was Jackson, my son, who provided the pivotal nudge.

"Can't you just stay with us Daddy?"

Those words struck a chord deep within me, it was all I needed to hear.

"Drive the car," I said to Tori as I climbed in for the last time. She understood the implication of my words, and though she tried to interject, her resistance was short-lived. The engine's purr marked my moment of surrender, and as the car moved forward, relief washed over me. But as the scenery blurred past the window, a sense of regret began to creep in. Too late now, I thought, the decision had been made.

Astonishingly, just a little farther down the road, I discovered that both Johann and Greg were only a few hours ahead of me. It was almost a revelation – during those hours of fatigue-induced haze, I had imagined them gaining insurmountable ground. If only I hadn't been so close to breaking, I might have been able to narrow the gap. What I failed to comprehend then was that everyone, even the more experienced racers, was grappling with the same struggles. Those who understood the rhythm of these ultra-marathons knew that the struggle was part of the journey. They anticipated moments of slowdown, embraced walking stretches, and persisted even when running seemed impossible. I had yet to grasp this valuable wisdom. My perception was skewed – I had mistaken walking for weakness and failure when, in truth, it was an integral strategy in these gruelling races.

For the next couple of days, we followed the race at a leisurely pace, in the comfort of the car, stopping along the way for a bit of sightseeing or to stretch our legs. While I was no longer in the race, I cheered on the other runners and observed Greg's remarkable victory and course record. After the race, Greg invited us to have dinner with his family at their stunning home before we headed back to the UK. During our visit, I seized the opportunity to glean insights from Greg's experience as a Team USA 24 hour runner– how he managed to rebound from a DNF at the previous years Vol State and run so resolutely this time around. I was hoping to take heart from his experiences to help inspire me for the World 24-hour Championships later that year. It impressed me that Greg had been running 200 mile weeks leading up to the race and this reaffirmed my belief in my own high volume training approach

Beyond running, Greg is a teacher in a Christian school and a driving force behind Run4Water, a mission committed to providing clean water solutions through funds generated from his running endeavours. A great runner and a great man, Greg truly inspired us all.

After Vol State, our journey led us to the Smoky Mountains. While driving through, an unexpected encounter stopped our car – a mother bear with her cubs crossing the road. The safety of our vehicle was a reassuring buffer, but this wildlife spectacle was a thrilling moment, especially for the children. It reminded me of the irreplaceable value of family moments over any race. If I had pressed on in the race, we would never have shared that unforgettable experience. It served as a poignant reminder, not that I needed any more, of the paramount importance of my family. My decisions to DNF held no regrets.

Shortly after the race, I received an email from Laz, where he highlighted that there were a few things going against me that meant it would be very difficult for me to finish. I assume he was alluding to the presence of my family and how it would have been incredibly challenging to continue while knowing they were nearby. Laz's own wife had shared stories with Tori of how, in his younger days, she and their children were his companions on his epic cross-country runs. I had to agree, having my family with me undoubtedly made it easier to make the tough call to stop. But now I was struggling to finish races with and without them being there.

Laz proclaims that Vol State is much more than a mere ultramarathon, a sentiment echoed by all who participate. Without the unexpected acts of kindness from road angels, I can only speculate how drastically more brutal the experience might have been. These small gestures were my lifelines whilst still in the race, propelling me on. It's not just the humidity and heat that crushes the spirit. The hills are brutal at times and when you combine a never-ending uphill slog with the extreme humidity it takes a strong will to see the funny side.

Reflecting on the race, I do wonder whether I would have pressed on had it not been for the debilitating chafing, was the chafing just the excuse I was looking for, could I have gritted it out? Possibly. Had I known that the leaders weren't that far ahead would it have pushed me to endure longer? Probably. However, sometimes you just have to admit that the course won.

Chapter 17

Albi Part 1

IN THE LEAD-UP TO THE WORLD 24-HOUR CHAMPION-
ships in Albi, France in October 2019, I was acutely aware that this
race needed to be my finest performance yet. It was a pivotal event
where the Team GB management team and selectors would be present,
and I'd be running alongside and against the entire current team,
presenting a golden opportunity to showcase my capabilities to those
I needed to impress. There was nowhere to hide; I couldn't simply
resign to the thought of throwing in the towel and just signing up
to another race if things got tough. This time, I had to give it my all.

The string of DNFs leading up to this event could have been
interpreted as a series of failures, they were, but leading up to race
day I chose to see them through a different lens. Rather than dwelling
on the missed targets in races like the Grand Union Canal Race,
Anglo-Celtic Plate, Vol State, and The Barry 40, I viewed them as
essential building blocks toward this pivotal race. The ultimate aim for

the year was securing qualification for Team GB, and accomplishing that would render the year a success, regardless of other outcomes.

In my preparatory notes, I scribbled motivational mantras, including "All failures this year were leading to this." And "It's only a day." While 24 hours seems like an eternity to be running, I had run for longer periods during my Spartathlon races. It was crucial to internalise that I was more than capable of enduring this time frame. Being part of Team GB's squad WhatsApp group – a collection of about 30 male and female runners who met specific standards in 24-hour running – due to my 235km performance at Belfast the prior year meant that I was on the selectors' radar. However, I knew I needed to achieve a big distance during this race to get onto the actual team and represent my country. My primary goal was 160 miles, with a secondary goal of 155 miles. Any distance between those benchmarks would likely meet the required standard.

In addition to honing my mental and physical preparedness, I delved into strategic planning, enlisting the help of my friend Hristo Tsvetkov from Bulgaria. Hristo, an accomplished ultrarunner with a penchant for detail due to his background as a computer programmer, was the perfect collaborator. Despite being in his early-20s, he held numerous national records and possessed an astute approach to racing that melded seamlessly with his technical acumen. Together, we constructed a comprehensive spreadsheet that outlined targeted paces for different segments of the race. Armed with this data, I entered the competition with a reassuring sense of confidence in my goals. The plan wasn't meant to be executed to the letter throughout the entirety of the event. That would suit some runners but for me it would become too stressful. It would act as a mental reference point against which I could gauge my performance and how the race was going. If I found myself maintaining paces in proximity to those outlined in the plan, I could rest assured that my race was on track.

I embraced a novel strategy of incorporating planned walking breaks, a tactic I hadn't employed before. Many elite 24-hour runners advocate for these intermittent pauses. Walking breaks, when strategically placed, can be advantageous. They provide an opportunity to use different muscles, allowing the running muscles to rest a little, following the walking phase, the body often feels reinvigorated for the next running stretch. By integrating calculated walking breaks before fatigue sets in, the idea is to pre-emptively manage exhaustion so that I was choosing beforehand when I would walk for a few minutes rather than being reduced to walking for hours through no choice of my own, as I had done at Vol State and GUCR.

The margins are so fine in a 24-hour. The ultimate aim is to stay out on the course and continue moving, attempting to maintain a viable running pace beyond the 20-hour mark. Although the pace is likely to slow as the race goes on, strategic walking breaks and a steady initial pace will conserve energy leaving a bit extra in the tank when the final few hours approach. I wanted to replicate the finishing experience of the Belfast 24 where I was overtaking runners, I spent months in the leadup to Albi visualising this exact scenario.

The significance of this event was inescapable - no room for retreat, no margin for excuses. The stakes were high, and I was ready to rise to the challenge.

My Mum and Stuart had flown over to France to look after the kids for a couple of nights so that Tori and I could solely focus on the race. Having my whole family nearby added a layer of comfort that diffused the pressure and calmed the racing nerves. Tori would be there with me during the race, I'd see her every mile as I went past the crew stations, I knew that with her support and encouragement, I'd be pushed to see this through.

The lead-up to the race was marked by intensive training and meticulous planning. One nagging uncertainty, however, lingered in my mind. 5 Weeks earlier I'd run an 80k ultra in the Bulgarian mountains. Initially running shoulder to shoulder with a Spanish skyrunning champion, I knew I'd gone off too fast, what was meant to be an enjoyable 'training run' had turned into a race. I pushed hard on the uphill sections but then struggled on the downhills as I always do, when I did attempt to run hard downhill on a particularly technical section, I fell smashing my knee into the rocks. I tried to get up and keep moving but it was obvious this was going to slow me down. Suddenly the distance remaining seemed quite intimidating; 40 miles in terrain this technical and rugged would be like 80 miles on the flat.

"Just get to the next aid station" I told myself, reasoning that the decision would be made for me there. My leg was covered in blood and my knee had already ballooned to twice its size. They would surely pull me from the race and I could go home. It turns out, Bulgarian aid station workers are less bound by health and safety concerns than their counterparts in the UK. As soon as I arrived at the aid station a guy filled my water bottles, sprayed my knee, patched it up and sent me on my way, "You go! You go! You will be fine."

As I kept moving the pain in my knee started to fade as other parts of my legs and feet started hurting. From being certain I was going to pull out I was determined to get to the end. I knew I wouldn't be quick and I certainly wouldn't place high in the field but it was time to put the DNFs behind me and prove I could tough it out, which is exactly what I'd have to do in five weeks' time if things didn't go to plan. It wasn't easy to keep going on such a brutal course, the relentless descents seemed designed to challenge my mental fortitude, as others breezed past with enviable agility. I tried to step lightly to avoid further jarring of my knee, but it got harder to do as I got more and more tired. Those climbs just kept coming as well. Just when I thought I was nearing the summit there was another sharp ascent. I was hurting but I was finishing, no matter what.

Darkness fell upon the course, I hadn't planned on finishing in the dark. Over 12 hours since I'd started, I crossed the finish line, broken but triumphant. It was a battle reminiscent of that first 50-mile race back in The Gower, a battle of willpower and determination. I'd broken the DNF habit.

After the race I could barely walk for a week let alone run. My knee had swollen up and was so stiff it was almost impossible to get moving, this unplanned pause allowed my body to recover from the taxing race along with the previous 150 mile training weeks . The week off did me no harm at all and I was able to bounce back with two weeks at 180 miles per week. This was a much-needed confidence boost as I headed to France.

The anticipation building up to the world 24-hour championships in Albi was electric. I couldn't wait to get started and as I watched the opening ceremony it was all the motivation I needed to see the GB squad walking around the track with their flag. I wanted to be standing alongside them next time around, a dream that felt within reach if everything unfolded as planned. I wished the team well and chatted a little with Dan Lawson, Dan is a great guy as well as an amazing runner, he's someone that lives his life on his own terms, this resonated deeply with me. He and his wife Charlotte home schooled their children and live a simple life that allows him to focus on his running and his family. His ability to balance his passion for running with family life and travel exemplified the way I aspired to live. Dan's prowess as a runner only deepened my respect, his name engraved on numerous course records and fastest known times.

I also managed to catch up with Greg Armstrong, my friend from Vol State, as well as other friends I had made from all over the world through my running adventures. As I walked to the Team USA tent with Greg I felt a little starstruck stood next to possibly the greatest female ultra runners to have ever lived, Camille Herron and Courtney Dauwalter, both of these wonderful athletes had been shattering any stereotype about gender in ultrarunning. Their feats had already become legends, and both were capable of clinching the overall victory.

As race day dawned, I understood the need to focus entirely on my own performance. My nutrition strategy had evolved, I would take a gel every 40 minutes, regardless of whether I felt sick or not. The idea of relying solely on gels for sustenance during a 24-hour race felt odd, but the mantra of "It's only a day" reassured me. Just as we can survive less-than-optimal diets for a day, the gels were my fuel in this intensive day-long battle. Combining gels, well-timed walking breaks, steady hydration, and controlled pacing formed my formula for success. In life as in running, goals demanded strategy. Flexibility was key, but staying true to the plan was imperative if I was to achieve my goal.

I was a little underweight going into Albi, which was due to the volume of my training no doubt, but I had become a lot less strict with my diet than I had been at times. If one of the children offers me a piece of chocolate I'll have it, and if I really fancy a bit of cake I won't beat myself up about it, but I do eat healthily most of the time. My usual weight is around 67kg and going into Albi I was just under 63kg so I was definitely feeling light on my feet. If I'm pushing 70kg I tend to feel it in my runs, they start to feel harder. It was intriguing to learn from my chats with Steve Way that he approached some races after his winter off-season around 10kg overweight, he thought it helped him feel really light when then losing all that weight for his goal races, 'train heavy - race light', it made sense.

The starting moment arrived, and I was keen to channel my adrenaline into focus. Surrounded by the world's top 24-hour runners, the atmosphere buzzed with energy. Amid the excitement, I reminded myself of my goal - to complete the race within the 155-160 mile range, not to chase after podium positions. I understood that if I attempted to keep pace with the frontrunners from the very beginning, I risked tiring prematurely, leaving me slogging through the latter hours of the event. My strategy was clear: I aimed to find my optimal rhythm and pace. I mentally grounded myself, ready to step onto the track and embrace the challenge that lay ahead.

I found my rhythm early on, slipping into a comfortable pace. The goal was to shut out the noise in my head, focusing solely on executing my strategy. However, the unfolding events on the track offered a stark lesson in determination. A runner surged past me with the most horrific stench, it became apparent that something had gone terribly wrong, brown liquid drenching their legs. I exchange glances with some of the other runners around us, none of us wanting to show any disgust. The runner's coach urged them to leave the track to clean up, frantically screaming "Get off the track; we need to hose you down! The officials have been complaining."

"No, I'm not getting off the track!"

"We need to get you off the track!"

the race referees got involved and forced the runner off the track to clean up, the runner displaying the kind of unyielding commitment required at the top level of sport. It was a vivid reminder of the less glamorous side of ultra-running, it showed me exactly how single-minded, unashamed, and driven I might have to be if I wanted to get to the very top.

As the nauseating smell eventually faded, I pressed on, battling the occasional twinge in my previously injured knee. Tori's encouragement boosted my spirits each time I passed her. Around me, I observed the performance of other runners, assessing my position against fellow GB competitors. While I was holding my ground, there was a long way to go.

Reaching the 50-mile mark, I was meeting my targets, but my legs ached. Nausea struck again, but this time I persisted through it. At the 100k point, my legs felt trashed, so I decided to sit down, never a great idea in a race.

"You Ok, Nath?" asked Tori.

"Yeah, I feel ok but my legs, they're just hurting."

At no point did I even think about quitting, not this time!

I started to punch my legs. To an outsider, it would look like I was having some kind of breakdown but I've found this to be quite effective. Tori rubbed my calves with a flannel. I've never really been one for a massage during or even post races but this really worked wonders! As soon as I got back on the track it was like I had new legs.

Amid the race, I spotted friends. Dan Masters from the Ham & Lyme 100k, was representing Canada and battling through a tough patch. Camille Herron's astounding pace left me awestruck. My friend David Bone moved with a perpetual smile, embodying the sheer joy of the experience. In these fleeting moments between strides, I felt the camaraderie of the ultra-running community, a collection of individuals united by their passion for this relentless sport.

Amidst the enjoyment, a fierce determination fuelled my strides. Achieving the qualifying standard was a non-negotiable goal, and anything short of that would feel like a letdown. But as I navigated the course, Tori's presence served as a reminder of the bigger picture. Family, love, and life's precious moments would always overshadow the outcomes of any race. Yet, this was a goal I had been striving for, a mark of achievement that held significance in my journey. And so, I summoned every ounce of my strength, determined to leave nothing behind on that track.

The race's nature is such that even the front-runners can only plan to run their best, not necessarily to win. The dynamics of a 24-hour race are unique, a true test of endurance both physically and mentally. The toll it takes on the body is substantial, and the aftermath often comes with peculiar reactions – night sweats and shivers that linger for days.

As the laps continued to roll by, each one a step closer to my goal, I held onto my strategy. I embraced the discomfort, welcomed the pain, and focused on maintaining a rhythm. The track's familiarity became comforting, my body's movement on the loop a dance between exertion and endurance. With the hours slipping away, I willed myself to push on, drawing strength from the cheers of the spectators, the camaraderie of fellow runners, and the unwavering support of Tori.

The race ebbed and flowed, moments of triumph interspersed with moments of struggle. The knee pain returned, but I forged ahead. I reminded myself that the journey, both on and off the track, is filled with peaks and valleys. The night brought its own challenges, the darkness amplifying both the physical and mental battles. But I embraced the night, finding solace in the moonlight and the rhythmic thud of my footsteps on the track.

I dug deep, tapping into reserves I didn't know I had. The pain was all-encompassing, but so was the determination. I was running not just for myself, but for every step that had brought me here, for every race, every setback, every victory, and every challenge overcome.

One of the best perks of doing these massive races is that for a short time afterward I just allow myself to be 'Fat Nathan' again. For a few days, I might polish off an entire tub of Haribo in a day or demolish a full container of ice cream, the kids love it when 'Fat Nathan' moves in. I'll have a few beers too, pretty much anything goes. My regular drinks are mostly black coffee or green tea, and these days I find myself hankering for healthy foods more often, so a little bit of junk food after a big race effort is a nice treat and doesn't do any harm.

These post-race feasts remind me that unless you're genetically inclined towards a slower metabolism or dealing with certain health conditions, managing weight largely boils down to diet and exercise. You don't have to go to the extremes I did initially. Just by integrating regular walks, cutting down on sugar-packed treats, and reining it in on ultra-processed foods, you can make significant strides in your well-being.

There did come a point in the race when I finally got sick of gels and decided to head to the official aid station to see what was on offer.

"You want yoghurt?" asked one of the volunteers.

Yoghurt was the last thing I expected. Glancing at what he was holding, it looked like a Mr. Whippy ice cream, but it was actually a cup of yoghurt buried beneath a generous mound of sugar. Honestly, it looked off-putting, but with no time for second thoughts, I thanked him and took it, savouring bites of sugar as I kept moving.

The initial bite made me cringe, but the expression on my face transformed in an instant. Surprisingly, it was delicious! Moreover, it injected a newfound vigour into my weary body. Maybe it was a sugar rush of epic proportions, but I'm sure the yoghurt played its part too. It was a concoction that worked wonders – a winning combination that I'd recommend to anyone. Although, perhaps just sitting down and gobbling it up without having run a substantial distance might not have the same effect.

At around 14 and a half hours the 100-mile mark came into view, the sugary yoghurt had revitalised me. I found out that I was leading the open race, I hadn't realised before and I really didn't care, it was irrelevant, all that mattered was staying out on that track and achieving my dream of qualifying to run for Great Britain. Slipping my headphones on, I was ready to dive into the final, critical stretch of the race. The only mantra echoing in my mind was "Just keep moving forward."

Chapter 18

Albi, Part 2

WHAT STRUCK ME PROFOUNDLY DURING ALBI WAS witnessing Greg Armstrong's dedication to cheering on the rest of us, even after his own race hadn't gone to plan and ended early. I knew Greg was a selfless individual, but his actions that day left me even more inspired. He must have harboured big ambitions for the race, given the extensive training he put in, and his injury-enforced withdrawal must have been disappointing. Yet, without missing a beat, he was out there, urging us all forward towards our goals.

As the clock ticked past the 16-hour mark, I decided to integrate squats into my walking breaks to keep my legs from locking up. Physically, I was holding up quite well, but the final 3rd of the race is notorious for unravelling the best of runners in an event like this. So, keeping my legs mobile was crucial to prevent any unwanted seizing up. It all boiled down to nailing the basics – a gel every 40 minutes, staying properly hydrated, and avoiding pushing the pace. It became a metronome-like rhythm, an intense mental battle as much as a physical one. This might be why some runners' races fall apart in the final stretch. Running for a full day is an immense challenge, and as you sense the finish line inching closer, your brain subconsciously sends signals to your body that it's almost time to relax. It's a risky mental game; the body feels tired so negative thoughts creep in, negative thoughts make the body feel weaker, the body feels weaker and the mind deteriorates further. The "It's only a day" mantra came back to me time and time again. I just had to keep pushing.

The 20-hour mark arrived, and I calculated that I was comfortably 10 to 15km ahead of the second-placed runner in the open category. The lead was substantial enough that the wheels would have to come flying off for someone to take my position. However, my primary focus wasn't about maintaining 1st place; I could be overtaken 2 or 3 times and I wouldn't care as long as I hit that elusive qualifying standard. I was clocking 9-minute miles, lapping struggling runners along the way. Overtaking anyone at any time does wonders for morale, but overtaking competitors more than 20 hours into a 24-hour race is an absolute spirit booster. Still, I reminded myself not to get too carried away. Everything could still fall apart and there was more chance of that happening if I tried to force the pace too soon.

As the clock ticked down to just an hour left, I briefly pulled up alongside Tori, who delivered a message from Hristo back in Bulgaria: "Now's the time to push on – you could run a great distance if you really get moving." I contemplated this for a moment but it didn't quite feel like the time. I chose to go against Hristo's advice for now and keep moving at the same pace for a few more laps. I was feeling strong but there was still an hour to go and if I went hard too early I could end up running less distance overall.

With just under 40 minutes remaining, the moment finally arrived. I took a deep breath and engaged the accelerator, instantly feeling like I was flying. To an onlooker, the change might have seemed subtle, perhaps going from 9-minute miles to 8:30-minute miles – but I seemed to be overtaking almost every runner in the field and it felt like I was moving really fast. The best part? It felt sustainable, like I had finally mastered the pacing for a 24-hour race. Robbie Britton, an elite ultra runner and coach, and now part of the Team GB management, had previously shared with me his almost flawless strategy from a past world 24-hour championship – overtaking relentlessly in the final hours after maintaining a steady pace throughout. I thought of Robbie as I attempted to replicate his strategy.

As the minutes dwindled, I checked my watch 154 miles with a few minutes left, I quickly calculated that to be around 247km, the qualifying standard was set at 245km. I had done it.. This might not guarantee a spot on the team as others could still run further between now and the selection window closing but I had done exactly what I had set out to accomplish. The finish was tantalisingly close, and I was yearning to be done. I was exhausted, but that fatigue was mixed with the sheer elation of having achieved my goal..

Hearing the siren that signalled the finish, I lay on the floor and waited for Tori who I knew wouldn't take too long to come along to pick me up. My body screamed for rest, and I had no intentions of moving anytime soon. Mission accomplished! My final distance – 248.655 km – translated to just a whisker under 155 miles and the added bonus of winning the open race.

As I lay there, chest heaving, legs trembling, I understood that this journey was not just about one race. It was about the relentless pursuit of a goal, the resilience to face setbacks, and the courage to push through pain. It was about the unwavering support of loved ones, the camaraderie of fellow runners, and the unbreakable spirit that propels us forward.

"Excuse me, Monsieur!" a local voice interrupted my exhausted thoughts.

I raised my head, mustering a weary smile. "You come for drug test," the official stated matter-of-factly.

Those two words hit me like a punch in the gut, knocking the air out of me. Instantly, a thousand negative thoughts flooded my mind. What if I had inadvertently taken a supplement that contained a banned substance? What if I had been unknowingly spiked? What if the seemingly innocuous yogurt from the aid station was some sort of cruel ruse and these officials were in on it? My fatigued brain conjured up a whirlwind of paranoid scenarios. While I hadn't done anything wrong, I still felt worried. I had never anticipated being drug-tested.

I hadn't wanted to be on my feet again so soon and just for a second I even contemplated refusing the drug test even though I knew that would rule me out of consideration for Team GB and would see the win taken off me, plus I'd look like a drugs cheat.

"Drug test?" the official repeated, urging me to move.

With reluctance, I heaved myself up from the ground, struggling to believe that mere moments ago, I was charging at 8:30-minute miles. However, as soon as the race had finished, my legs had immediately decided their work was done, and every bit of stiffness, heaviness, and pain came to the surface. My movement was akin to a tin man in dire need of oil, while the official seemed to be sprinting ahead.

A bottle was handed to me, but not before I had queued for around 30 minutes. Winners from other categories were similarly lined up – including Camille Herron, who had broken the world record and seized victory in the women's race, ahead of her nearest rival by 16 km. Now, she sat in a wheelchair, being wheeled toward a drug test, a stark reminder of the unseen side of ultra-running. It was undeniable that these long-distance races took an immense toll on the body, underscoring the importance of proper recovery.

My immediate concern, however, had a different focus. Running 155 miles almost guaranteed dehydration, regardless of my best efforts. And despite trying relentlessly, I found myself unable to pee.

"You will have to drink some water," I was informed, and so I did, downing bottle after bottle. But still, my bladder refused to comply! This was excruciating! All I wanted to do was go and collapse on my bed back at the hotel but it didn't seem that would be happening any time soon. Minutes crept by sluggishly, and I kept sipping water, unfortunately, drug tests couldn't be conducted on vomit, or else I would have been out of there when it seemed as though all the water I'd been guzzling down the past hour violently hurled from my mouth.

What started as mild annoyance was now becoming stressful. I was no longer concerned about what the test might unearth; I was simply furious that I couldn't pee. This was proving harder than the race itself.

Nearly two hours dragged on before my body decided to cooperate once more. As the liquid finally flowed, I experienced nothing short of pure joy and relief. The officials seemed satisfied, but it would be several weeks before the test results arrived, of course they were negative. My recollections of getting back to the hotel were hazy at best, and I eventually woke up, soaked in sweat. Oh, the glamour!

Mum and Stuart brought Skye, Summer, and Jackson along to the post-race ceremony, I'll always remember that look of pride on all their faces as they watched me approach the stage to claim my trophy. I'd hoped the drawn-out proceedings hadn't bored them too much, considering they endured the presentation of several awards before mine. But finally, after an hour of anticipation, I hobbled up to the stage to retrieve my prize. As I clutched the trophy, a triumphant grin spread across my face, I'd done it.

The overall winner, Aleksandr Sorokin of Lithuania, stood tall at the top of the podium, having covered 173 miles. Given his track record his victory wasn't much of a surprise to anyone. The gap between his performance and the legendary Yiannis Kouros' 24-hour world record was similar to the gap between my distance and his at Albi, although, I am confident that Aleksandr will one day break that elusive 24 hour record. (*2023 - Aleksandr Sorokin now holds the world record for 24 hour running, it stands at 319.614 km achieved during the 2022 IAU 24-Hour European Championships in Verona, Italy)

In these ultra-races, our goals are deeply personal, and while they can't always be achieved, when they are, a sense of accomplishment is undeniable. On the flip side, when we fall short, it becomes an opportunity to introspect and figure out what could have been done differently.

The timeline that spanned less than five years – from struggling to cover a mile to conquering 155 miles in 24 hours – didn't unfold due to some innate talent I possessed. No, it was driven by two pivotal ingredients that hold the recipe for achieving great things in life: unyielding belief and unrelenting hard work. To represent your country in any sport requires serious dedication. Granted, the path may be riddled with unique obstacles that some face and others don't. I was fortunate that Tori stood beside me, understanding, and nurturing my aspirations. Fortunate that my lifestyle allowed me to dedicate myself to the daily grind of running, even though it was a lifestyle built on conscious choices. Most of us possess a choice in how we spend our time. Luck played its part in keeping me free from significant injuries during training. The list could go on, but at the heart of it, I achieved something that is within the realm of possibility for many.

I never want my children to be limited in their ambition. While I won't push them toward pursuits that won't bring them happiness, I do hope that they see in my story a testament to the attainability of their dreams. The same goes for each of my coaching clients. My own journey has been a treasure trove of learning, and I aspire to continue guiding others to unlock the same lessons.

For now though, I would just have to wait until I got the call to tell me if I'd achieved my goal of being selected to run for Great Britain. I had done all I could, it was now in the hands of the selectors.

Chapter 19:

India

AS THE WHEELS OF THE PLANE TOUCHED DOWN IN
Mumbai, I knew that our winter adventure in India was about to
begin. Fresh from the Albi 24-hour race, the excitement of a new
journey mingled with the fatigue still lingering in my muscles. The
plan was simple: immerse ourselves in a different culture, experience
life beyond our comfort zone, and, of course, lace up my running
shoes for some Indian trails.

But right from our first steps on the vibrant streets of Mumbai,
a wave of culture shock hit us like a splash of cold water. In the
midst of this bustling metropolis, we found ourselves stepping over
a homeless family with a new-born baby, nestled on the pavement.
The impact of this sight struck deep within us all. It was as if reality
had thrown us a curveball, testing our emotions and our reasons
for being here.

There was quite a sombre atmosphere in our hotel on the first
night. Poverty, an unfortunate reality in India, had made its presence

known to us in an unignorable way. When you spend more time in somewhere like Mumbai sights like this become more commonplace, I wouldn't say we got desensitised to them but the level of poverty did become less of a shock on our travels through India..

A few days laters amidst the whirlwind of Mumbai I received a call from Kiran, a local woman known for running the 'Marathons of India' website. She had caught wind of my success at Albi and wanted to interview me. Coffee and conversation awaited me at the luxurious Taj Mahal Palace hotel, a setting that seemed almost incongruous with my running gear.

Sitting across from Kiran, I felt at ease despite the grandeur of the place. We were joined by Breeze Sharma, India's best known ultra runner and mountaineer whose achievements could fill volumes. This was the man who had stood atop the world's highest peaks, including Everest and run some pretty tough ultras including Death Valley's gruelling Badwater. Breeze had wanted to meet me, I had no idea why, my accomplishments paled in comparison to his, I was honoured to meet him.

Breeze has a fascinating story, growing up in a small Indian village and then discovering mountaineering when he joined the navy. He was introduced to running by another naval colleague and is now a Red Bull sponsored athlete. Reaching the top of Everest came at a price, the time at extreme altitude having an impact on his fitness that took a long time to recover from, but some of his best achievements came after he finally got his lung capacity back.

As I engaged in conversation with Kiran and Breeze, it was like finding an oasis of familiarity in the midst of the unknown. It was a reminder that no matter where life takes you, the shared language of passion and pursuit can bridge even the widest cultural gaps. But time marches on, and soon it was time for my family to leave Mumbai behind, embarking on a 26-hour train journey to Rajasthan.

That train ride was an adventure in itself. Plates of fragrant curry were served, a burst of flavour and culture in the confined space of our tiny cabin. The kids, Tori, and I soaked in the adventure, cherishing each moment as the train carried us further into the heart of India.

Our Indian escapade was teaching us what embracing the journey truly meant. From the shock of stark inequality to the comfort of conversation in grand hotels and the thrill of train travel. As the landscape of India unfolded before us, I realised that it's never about the finish line; it's about every step of the way.

Kiran and Breeze, with their well-connected friends, had orchestrated quite the welcome for us in Jaipur. I couldn't help but chuckle at how swiftly our journey had transitioned from the sombre contemplation of Mumbai's streets to the kaleidoscope of invitations and unexpected experiences in Rajasthan.

Jaipur greeted us with open arms, and we found ourselves on the guest list for a party hosted by the President of Rajasthan, flanked by the vibrant Jaipur runners' community. The prospect of a TV interview added a dash of thrill to the mix. I figured it might be exciting and amusing for the kids to see Dad on TV and, quite honestly, an entertaining escapade for all of us.

We were made to feel extremely welcome and were all invited up onto the stage where we were each gifted one of the local turbans to wear. The absurdity of the situation wasn't lost on me – there I was, a Welshman wearing a traditional turban in India. It was a sight that could have made a comedy sketch. I chuckled inwardly, especially as I looked over at Tori and the kids all kitted out in the local attire.

However, my chuckles were momentarily swallowed as my gaze landed on the stage backdrop. In bold letters, it read, "Jaipur welcomes Nathan Flear, World 24-hour Champion." A pang of nervousness jolted in my stomach. A whispered conversation with Tori confirmed my suspicion – there had been a mix-up. They assumed my victory in the open race at Albi translated to a world championship title. Kiran and Breeze must have thought the same, hence the interview offer and Breeze's eagerness to meet me, he had thought he was meeting a world champion.

The cameras were rolling, and there I was, contemplating my next move. Should I correct this on live TV and risk causing a cringe-worthy scene? I could already envision the headlines: "Flear's Faux Pas: A Champion Only in His Dreams." The spotlight was on me, and not just metaphorically. I took a deep breath and decided to roll with it, hoping they wouldn't explicitly mention the supposed world championship.

The interviewer seemed to have a knack for fitting those two words – world champion – into every other sentence. Each utterance felt like a neon sign flashing behind me, declaring my inadvertent fib to the world. My mind raced, conjuring scenes of runners from around the globe scratching their heads, wondering when I had ascended to world champion status.

I deflected as best I could, weaving responses that gently set the record straight without bringing the spotlight crashing down on this well-intentioned event. "You know," I'd say, "since I wasn't running for my country in this particular race, I competed in the open race and, well, that was the race I had won. But, fingers crossed, I'll be donning my national colours at the next world championships."

Still, the interviewer persisted, bestowing upon me the "world champion" title with an insistence that matched the rhythm of a ticking clock. I kept downplaying it, steering clear of exposing the misunderstanding like a diplomat sidestepping a landmine. I hoped they sensed the correction between the lines, perhaps understanding that my crown was more like a feather in the cap.

Once the interview concluded, a collective sigh of relief swept over me. Yet, the lingering unease remained. I hoped the members of Jaipur running club wouldn't feel duped if they caught on to the truth. I mulled over scenarios – maybe they actually did know, and the "world champion" was a playful euphemism for open race winner. But either way, to the Jaipur crew, if you're reading this, my friends, please accept my apologies for any confusion!

However, the camaraderie and warmth of the Jaipur runners eased any lingering discomfort. They embraced us like old friends, and their kindness extended beyond the party lights. When Summer developed a tooth infection, a member of the club who happened to be a doctor swooped in to arrange a visit to a private dentist. Believe me, navigating medical issues in India was a labyrinthine challenge that I was immensely grateful to sidestep.

That quirky interview remained as a playful reminder that life has its share of hilariously unexpected moments. In the midst of cultural immersion, a misplaced title, and friendships forged through running, we laughed, connected, and embraced the journey, quirks and all.

Running through Goa, with its jungles and sandy shores, felt like stepping into a runner's dream. If paradise had a flavour, it was the taste of the sea, the warmth of the sun, and the harmony of jungle sounds enveloping you. Goa had this enchanting way of awakening my inner explorer, and so I embarked on early morning escapades, racing the dawn to uncover the hidden corners of this tropical haven.

Through Dan Lawson I met a local guy, Pem, we ran together, Pem had gone to a Buddhist school in the Himalayas and was a huge advocate of plyometrics and yoga. He held classes on movement, all great stuff for a runner and running coach to learn. Running alongside him was like watching a yogi on a jog. He could twist his body into shapes that defied reason. I spent hours watching Pem move and gleaning as much as I could from his knowledge of movement.

My quest for knowledge was insatiable. India was my classroom, and I was the eager student with a thirst for learning. Kenya had been all about learning from the greatest marathon runners and coaches in the world and how I could make adjustments to get more out of my training, which I could then impart to others. India was about learning additional bits of health-based knowledge that I could bring into my life.

Health isn't just about keeping your engine well-oiled; it's about understanding the mechanics, the secret codes that keep it humming. There's a treasure trove of health practices scattered across the globe, like little gems waiting to be uncovered. Take China, for instance, where age seems to be just a number for the spry and healthy elderly. India had this mystique about it, like an ancient library of wellness secrets waiting to be unravelled.

Ayurvedic medicine had always piqued my curiosity, and the Himalayas held the key. So, spending a month in Rishikesh with the mountains as my backdrop, I enrolled in a course with a local Ayurvedic doctor. I had a huge interest in natural methods of healing and I have various herbs I use for recovery along with different herbal teas., my cabinets are stacked with natural concoctions for better recovery and relaxation. Sure, during a 24-hour race, I might guzzle down a staggering number of energy gels, but day to day, I try to keep things as unprocessed as I can.

One herb that had caught my attention was ashwagandha. It sounded like the secret password to a hidden treasure chest of energy and recovery. Being completely legal I added it to my arsenal, hoping to give my endurance a natural herbal boost. I spent hours every day with the Ayurvedic doctor, I immersed myself, soaking up as much knowledge as I could.

But the Indian trails had more surprises in store, including a chance encounter with psychologist Dr. Mark Slaski on a sun-kissed Christmas Day in Goa. The universe was apparently conspiring for this meeting, as our kids played together, Mark and I chatted away, he was very interested in my running and the races I had run and ended up writing an article about it which then led to the two of us appearing together on a podcast.

In the article, Mark explored what made the gears of my runner's mind tick. He had delved into the minds of "hardcore achievers" from business tycoons to entertainers. He even decided to add me to his list of these high-achieving minds. He talked about discipline, that battle between the allure of snooze buttons and the resolve to chase a goal. It's that moment when your alarm chirps, your body protests, and you must decide: bed or a 20-mile run? It's a delicate dance between fatigue and resolve, knowing when to push through and when to pamper your body.

Persistence also had its moment in the spotlight. Those Spartathlon races weren't all smooth sails; they had their moments of turbulence. When the road zigged instead of zagged, it was up to me to course correct. That ability to dig deep when the path gets rocky – that's what sets Spartathlon racers apart from the average bystander. And me? Well, let's just say I had a love-hate relationship with those low points as we saw from 2019, I wasn't immune from losing that mental battle from time to time.

Marks article suggested that Single-mindedness was the secret sauce. When I started running, my obsession level could've classified me as a running monk, a monomaniac with a sole focus. While that intensity might've been trying for those around me, it was the spark that ignited my journey. Today, the flame still burns, albeit in a more balanced glow. But having a goal isn't just about the destination; it's about the daily steps, the whispers to yourself that remind you where you're headed.

Mark and I became friends. Our conversations focussed on psychology and performance, unearthing gems of insight that I would use to help me become a better runner and that I now weave into my coaching sessions when working on mindset and motivation with my athletes. I love to learn and gain knowledge, India was teaching me a lot.

Something else that intrigued me was Fasting. Fasting is a big part of some aspects of Indian culture, such as Buddhism and Ayurvedic medicine, and so I decided to conduct a little experiment during part of our time there. The medical benefits are talked about along with endurance training benefits; I guess if you can teach your body to cope without food for a while it will only be of help in long distance running.

For three days, I chose to forgo solid food, just having water and cups of Ashwagandha herbal tea. My training routine continued – mornings and evenings running beneath the Indian sun, albeit with slightly reduced mileage compared to my peak training. There was this whisper that after two or three days of fasting, a mystical state of enlightenment might be reached. I wondered if I'd come out the other side as a Zen-like guru or merely a hungry runner.

Turns out, enlightenment wasn't on my itinerary. No spiritual awakening graced me with its presence. Instead, I just felt awful! I could feel the strength draining out of me as time went on and it got to the point where I would feel dizzy and faint during my runs. Reason slapped me in the face during the third day. I was out in India with Tori and the kids – this was not the time to be taking risks with my health. By the time I could eat again, relief washed over me like a tidal wave. We went out to our favourite restaurant in the jungle, the fast was well and truly broken.

I still remain curious about fasting's potential. Those who swear by it maintain that you really do feel like a different person afterwards and I am still intrigued to give it a proper go but it doesn't take a genius to work out that fasting and heavy endurance training probably shouldn't mix. How could I be telling the ultra team in Kenya to be eating three times as much as they normally would during training whilst eating nothing myself? I just don't believe that anything good can come from training in that overly fasted state.

Our time in India drew to a close. Just as Kenya had etched its lessons, so had India, in its own vibrant colours. We moved on to Thailand, promised luxury and leisure, a departure from the backpacking odyssey we'd undertaken. We found ourselves in a villa, complete with our own pool thanks to Jeff and Jane Strachan, friends we'd met at the Spartathlon, Jeff was Darren Strachan's brother, Daz my friend who had kindly crewed for me on that disastrous run on the Grand Union canal – Jeff and Jane had kindly given us the keys to their place and told us to stay as long as we liked.. It was paradise.

Yet as we basked in our Thai haven, the world outside continued to spin in an increasingly ominous direction. The Coronavirus pandemic, like a storm on the horizon, cast its shadow across the globe. News reports painted apocalyptic scenarios. Conversations with Tori after tucking the kids in took on a new weight. The virus, like an unwelcome ghost, seemed to lurk around every corner.

Mum and Stuart were on a cruise ship off the coast of South America, they would eventually be allowed to dock six weeks later. Parts of Europe were already on lockdown, we started to get a little concerned. What if we were stranded in Thailand? We made our exit while we could. Flights were rebooked, and our journey back to Bulgaria set in motion.

And so, India and Thailand became fond memories. The road ahead seemed uncertain.

Chapter 20:

Lockdown

TALK ABOUT TIMING! OUR PLANE'S WHEELS TOUCHED down on Bulgarian soil, and the very next day, the Bulgarian authorities announced a lockdown of our home town, the small mountain town of Bansko. Life as we knew it would shrink to fit within the confines of our homes. We would only be allowed to leave our homes once a day for groceries or essential trips out and even then we had to keep it very local. The outside world began to resemble scenes from an apocalyptic movie, with an air of uncertainty hanging heavy.

Yet amid the uncertainty, one thing seemed certain to be disrupted – my running routine. For five years, running had been my constant, an almost daily ritual that anchored my life. Now, stepping out for a run came with the prospect of being arrested. The temptation was there to slip out and take a forbidden jog, given that the local police seemed more likely to offer a cigarette than pursue a runner I was sure they wouldn't give chase, and even if they did

I fancied my chances of getting away. However, my family's safety was my priority and that kept me rooted at home.

The day of our return still allowed me to sneak in a run, but it wasn't as straightforward as I had imagined. We had arrived from a sun-soaked country to Bulgaria's mountain winter, greeted by a snowy landscape. We landed in shorts and t-shirts to find completely different scenes to when we had left for India. All our winter gear lay in suitcases packed away at an apartment down at the coast and all of the local clothes shops had been closed due to the lockdown. With creativity my only ally, I donned a couple of pairs of boxer shorts as makeshift gloves, wrapped another around my neck like a buff, and slid into a pair of Tori's leggings. I managed to survive the run without becoming a casualty of hypothermia, but little did we know that would be my last run outside for a good while.

Just as I had got back from my run, news broke – Bansko, our town, was going into full quarantine. The media cast Bansko as the new European epicentre of the virus, a label that didn't quite suit the picturesque mountain town. They blamed a British family for importing the virus, thankfully not the British family that had just flown in from Asia. This brought some awkward moments as our nationality suddenly came with an unwanted spotlight. "No English Allowed" signs adorned local grocery shops, it was disappointing, barricades sprang up around town, while holidaymakers were told to evacuate by midnight or face being marooned.

Initially, it was Bansko alone that was under lockdown but soon, the whole country followed suit. As the days unfolded, it was revealed that the English family in question hadn't actually tested positive for the virus, but by then, the die had been cast. For a while, it felt a little uneasy being British in Bansko,

Just weeks ago, I had been running through the jungles of Goa and Thailand. Now, we found ourselves confined to our Bulgarian apartment. The apartment complex's corridors became my running track. Running laps, up and down the corridor, a miniature racecourse right outside my front door. From outdoor trails to indoor corridors, from freedom to confinement. That hallway transformed into an arena of determination.

On one of those days, I decided to tackle a 50k run, all within the confines of that corridor. Recalling the tales I'd heard of 24-hour races held in abandoned shopping centres, I took up the challenge. It was a mental battle to keep running up and down that corridor for several hours, but when I neared our door I would hear the kids misbehaving the other side and think "Well maybe I'll just do a few more laps." Hearing the kids driving Tori mad behind our door, would encourage me to stay out there a little longer, Sorry, Tori! I plugged in my iPod, letting podcasts carry me through those uninspiring miles.

At the time I thought everything would blow over pretty quickly and my planned summer races would still be going ahead but as time went on it seemed there might be a longer wait in store. This became problematic as the corridor running was putting strains on my body. All of the stopping and starting along with the rapid turns were giving me a few niggles. After around six weeks of corridor running I decided to risk a dawn run into the forest at the foot of the mountains.

As I entered the woods, I found that I wasn't the only one daring to head outside. Locals greeted me with an air of familiarity. Their unhurried strides and casual nods spoke volumes – these woods had become their secret haven, a haven shared by silent pact every morning.

By June it was almost as if the whole thing had never happened, at least in Bansko, although things looked to be getting worse in the UK and elsewhere in the world. I managed a few local races over the summer and showed up to them having done mostly corridor running so I had no real expectations. With no pressure I performed better than expected. I won a six hour race, had a surprise podium finish in a fast 50k mountain race, and finished in the Top 10 in a competitive 100k mountain ultra. Race photos painted a consistent picture – me, smiling. The same smile that had graced my face when I had started running, when I was unburdened by expectations. With no pressure, I was enjoying my running again.

As the lockdown came to an end there was still a piece of news I was waiting to hear. Had I made the GB team? The selection window had now closed so any news, good or bad, could arrive any day. I'd missed out by a relatively small margin the year before. I was hoping this along with my performance at Albi would show the selectors that I was learning valuable lessons and making improvements. I also wondered if they would see past my string of 2019's DNF's. Would Albi's triumph be viewed as a fleeting flicker, a fluke? Was I really capable of running for Team GB? Was I really good enough? If I didn't make the cut I would try harder next time, I couldn't just give up on the dream.

Whatever happened I could reflect on the past five years and be proud of what I had achieved. I had started running to lose weight and get fit but with each small achievement the next goal just seemed a little more achievable, an invitation to continue to aim higher. I've always been quite a positive person, you must believe you can, or at least be willing to attempt. If you give it a go then who knows what might happen?

I wanted to write this book to show people what might be possible if they try. I believe that so much of what stops us from achieving things is a lack of self-belief. There is untapped potential within us all. If just one person finds inspiration from my story, if they can find that spark of possibility that smolders within us all, my time spent writing it would have been worth it. Embrace the journey of life, life is an adventure, believe in yourself, do what makes you happy!

My running journey has taken me from the trails to the roads, the mountains to the beaches, from disbelief to conquering, from setbacks to triumphs. Yours, too, can be a saga of transformation. And even as the world's uncertainties pose their challenges, remember that the heart of a runner beats with resilience, and the spirit of a dreamer soars above the obstacles that dare to stand in the way.

Epilogue

HALF A YEAR HAD PASSED SINCE THAT RACE IN ALBI. Yet, that day, lingered in my mind throughout. The thrill of the race, the cheers of the crowd, the taste of achievement – it all seemed both distant and vivid. And all the while, a question loomed: when would the call come?

Then one morning, after getting in from my run, I received a message from the Team GB manager John Pares, "Hi Nathan, would you be free for a call?" With eager anticipation mingled with trepidation, I replied, "Hi John, I'm free all day, feel free to call anytime".

Within a few minutes the phone rang, my heart raced in sync with its ringing tone. Around me, the expectant eyes of Tori, Skye, Summer, and Jackson fixed upon me. I was nervous, I don't really get nervous, I took a few seconds to gather myself before answering the phone.

"Hi Nathan," John's voice cut through the suspense. After a few pleasantries, John proceeded.

"Look Nathan, the standard was really high this year, which is of course great for the team, but I'm not going to beat about the bush. Your distance in Albi was good enough. You're in the team. Congratulations!"

Tori and the kids must have known from the look on my face that it was good news. They looked so happy for me, I still get emotional thinking about it. I thanked John but I can barely remember a thing that was said afterwards. I was just so overwhelmed with excitement, joy and most of all relief. My dream had now become reality.

I put down the phone and hugged my family.

The 2020 European Championships beckoned from Austria, a mere six months away. The path was clear – to train, to prepare, to give my all.

The kids baked me a celebratory Banana bread, my favourite. In its warmth, I tasted not just a sweet treat, but the culmination of years of striving, of pushing boundaries, and of finally realising the goals I had worked so hard to achieve.

As this special day came to an end, I pondered the road ahead. Team GB selection had been a mountain conquered, and yet, just beyond that peak lay another challenge I couldn't stop thinking about, another chance to test the limits of my potential. Now that I had achieved my goal, I needed another challenge. Could I go even farther? The British 48-hour record had stood for over 30 years – Could I try to break it and etch my name into the record books?

And so, as this chapter of my tale comes to a close, I hope you take with you the understanding that life is an unending journey of possibility. Dreams realised are stepping stones to dreams yet unimagined. As you close this book, let it not be an ending, but a springboard to your own adventures. I hope it inspires you to face challenges head-on, to savour your victories, and to embrace the twists that life presents us.

Remember, every finish line is just a new starting point, every triumph a foundation for greater heights.

Afterword

UNFORTUNATELY, THE EUROPEAN 24-HOUR CHAMPION-ships of 2020 found itself the victim the Covid-19 pandemic, an unwelcome guest that had already overstayed its welcome. The event was cancelled, leaving the hopes and aspirations of athletes like me shattered.

The cycle repeated the following year. The 2021 World championships, for which I had also been selected for, were set to take place in Timisoara, Romania, fell under the shadow of the same pandemic that had disrupted our plans once before. Another race cancelled; another opportunity missed.

Then, finally, in October 2022, The European 24-hour championships held in Verona, Italy. I got my chance, stood there, wearing the Team GB vest with pride. Tori, Skye, Summer, and Jackson stood by my side, witnesses to the culmination of years of dedication and unwavering pursuit. The proudest moment of my running career so far, no matter what happened in the future my children could always say that their dad reached the very pinnacle of his sport.

The journey was complete.... For now...

Acknowledgements

Thank you:

To my incredible family – Tori, Skye, Summer, and Jackson – for being the bedrock of my journey, your constant support and unwavering belief in my dreams have fuelled my pursuits. My heartfelt thanks extend to my mum and Stuart, whose encouragement has been a constant source of strength, thanks mum for being mum and dad throughout my childhood.

To every fellow runner who shared a start line or a training route with me, your camaraderie and shared passion have shaped this path in remarkable ways. To the race directors and cherished running companions who transformed the miles into memories, thank you for making this expedition a joyous one.

To the athletes I have had the privilege to coach and work with, your trust in my coaching philosophies has been both humbling and inspiring. Your determination mirrors my own journey's resilience, and I'm grateful to have played a part in your progress.

Lastly, to everyone who has crossed my path, leaving an indelible mark – your presence, no matter how fleeting, has contributed to my life's story. Every interaction, every shared moment, has propelled me forward.

Thank you for reading my book, I hope you can take some inspiration from my story.

Connect with Me

IF MY JOURNEY HAS RESONATED WITH YOU AND sparked a desire for your own transformation, I invite you to get in touch. Whether you're seeking personalised run coaching, looking to overcome hurdles with newfound motivation, or aiming to build a resilient mindset, I'm here to offer my support.

Feel free to reach out via my website www.nathanflear.co.uk Taking that first step can set you on the path to realising your aspirations. Remember, every remarkable journey begins with a single stride, and I'm here to walk alongside you as you work towards your goals.

Let's continue this adventure together. Your dreams are within reach, and I'd love to help you in turning them into reality.

Printed in Great Britain
by Amazon

40517252R00128